Aerial Warfare: A Very Short Introduction

Praise for the hardback: *Aerial Warfare: The Battle for the Skies*

'a superbly written short survey of the dilemmas, controversies, failures and successes of air power' and 'a refreshing and highly informative read'

Dr Vladimir Rauta, *Defence Studies*

'For a brief but comprehensive history of air power in war that does full justice to both its achievements and its controversies...one need look no further than this readable book'

Dr Ian Gooderson, Royal Air Force Chief of the Air Staff Reading List 2018

'One of the great air power textbooks, now and for the future'

Dr Brian Laslie, Deputy Command Historian, North American
Air Defense Command

VERY SHORT INTRODUCTIONS are for anyone wanting a stimulating and accessible way into a new subject. They are written by experts, and have been translated into more than 45 different languages.

The series began in 1995, and now covers a wide variety of topics in every discipline. The VSI library currently contains over 600 volumes—a Very Short Introduction to everything from Psychology and Philosophy of Science to American History and Relativity—and continues to grow in every subject area.

Very Short Introductions available now:

Available soon:

For more information visit our website

www.oup.com/vsi

Frank Ledwidge

AERIAL WARFARE

A Very Short Introduction

OXFORD
UNIVERSITY PRESS

OXFORD
UNIVERSITY PRESS

Great Clarendon Street, Oxford, OX2 6DP,
United Kingdom

Oxford University Press is a department of the University of Oxford.
It furthers the University's objective of excellence in research, scholarship,
and education by publishing worldwide. Oxford is a registered trade mark of
Oxford University Press in the UK and in certain other countries

© Frank Ledwidge 2020

The moral rights of the author have been asserted

First edition published in 2020
First published in hardback as *Aerial Warfare: The Battle for the Skies* 2018
First published as a *Very Short Introduction* 2020

Impression: 1

Published in the United States of America by Oxford University Press
198 Madison Avenue, New York, NY 10016, United States of America

British Library Cataloguing in Publication Data
Data available

Library of Congress Control Number: 2019955393

ISBN 978-0-19-880431-4

Printed in Great Britain by
Ashford Colour Press Ltd, Gosport, Hampshire

Links to third party websites are provided by Oxford in good faith and
for information only. Oxford disclaims any responsibility for the materials
contained in any third party website referenced in this work.

Contents

Acknowledgements

Over the course of researching and writing this book many people with great knowledge of air power and its history have given vital help. It is always difficult to do justice to everyone, but here goes.

My colleagues at RAF Cranwell have been superb, sharing their academic and operational knowledge. Dr Andrew Conway, Wing Commander (retd) Mal Craghill, Group Captain (retd) Chris Finn, Dr Carl Hartford, Dr Ben Jones, Dr Peter Lee, Sqn Ldr Aggi Morrison, Dr Steven Paget, Dr Matthew Powell, and Lt Col. Rob Spalton and Tim Dean were good enough to read all or part of the text and make corrections or suggestions, as was Dr Eitan Shamir of the Begin-Sadat Center in Israel. Professor Arthur Miller's insights into the history of stealth technology were fascinating. I'd also like to thank the superb library staff at Cranwell for their kindness, refuge, and good advice as well as Lucianne Hey and Nicola Beynon, whose calm organizational skills allow us all to work effectively. Dr Ed Burke and Dr Bettina Renz at Nottingham and Dr Vladimir Rauta at Reading were extremely helpful and kind. Colonel John Andreas Olsen, the doyen of professional air power scholarship, was characteristically extremely helpful and encouraging.

Shashank Joshi and Justin Bronk, two of the Royal United Services Institute's leading commentators and experts, looked over a section each, something beyond the call of duty, and I am very grateful.

I would also like to thank the anonymous reviewers for Oxford University Press and also the book's patient editor Jenny Nugee, the production team led by Ganesan Kayalvizhi, copy-editor Edwin Pritchard, and proofreader Rebecca Bryant. Everything they suggested was constructive and helpful and has made this a far better book. Where there are errors, they are mine.

I must also mention the RAF officers and officer cadets at Cranwell, the home of the Royal Air Force. I have learned a very great deal from them over the years and I have tried to incorporate some of that in this book. Their expertise has ranged from the complexities of layered air defences during the Cold War to how hand-held drones assist in contemporary combat.

The help and advice of all these remarkable people was invaluable; where mistakes have been made it is because I have ignored that advice.

Finally, my family—Nevi and James—have endured many evenings when I grumpily told them 'don't you know I've a book to write?' Enough of that for now!

List of illustrations

List of abbreviations and acronyms

As with most military topics, air power is replete with acronyms and abbreviations. The following are used in this book:

A2AD	Anti-Access Area Denial
AAR	air-to-air refuelling
ABM	Aerospace Battle Management
ACTS	Air Corps Tactical School
AEW	airborne early warning
AWACS	airborne [early] warning and control system
C2	command and control
C3	command, control, and communications
CAS	close air support
ECM	electronic countermeasures
FAA	Fuerza Aerea Argentina, the Argentine Air Force
GBAD	ground-based air defences
GPS	global positioning system
IADS	integrated air defence system
IAF	Israeli Air Force
IDF	Israeli Defence Forces
IS	Islamic State
JSTARS	joint surveillance target attack radar system
MEDEVAC	medical evacuation
NATO	North Atlantic Treaty Organization
NLF	National Liberation Front

Chapter 1
Foundations

Air power is 'the ability to use air capabilities in and from the air to influence the behaviour of actors and the course of events'; this Royal Air Force definition is as good as any. For decades air power has been the primary tool used by major powers to coerce recalcitrant opponents. Those 'air capabilities' are almost as likely to be wielded today by unmanned aircraft or a guided missile as they are by an aeroplane with a crew dropping bombs. The principles of the deployment, the grammar as it were of air power, have changed little over the last 100 years or so. Only the technology, the vocabulary, has altered. In 1918, oil-streaked aircrew in open cockpits flew fabric-covered biplanes over shell-pocked First World War battlefields. In 2018 their great-grandchildren, gazing at computer screens in cabins humming with technology, pilot drones over dusty villages thousands of miles away. The roles they carry out are broadly the same.

As a dominant, if not *the* dominant military technology over the last century, air power has developed extraordinarily quickly. In one sense, of course, aircraft are simply another military technology like firearms or submarines, both of which have greatly influenced military conflict. However, air power has several unique qualities. First, it has the potential of *ubiquity*. Giulio Douhet (1869–1930), one of the early 'prophets' of air power, wrote in 1919 that 'the airplane has complete freedom of action and direction; it can fly to and from any point of the compass in the shortest time—in a straight line—by any route deemed expedient'.

Secondly, it may do so at great *height* permitting extensive observation. Third, it has *reach* which applies over both land and sea; geographical obstacles are not relevant. Finally, aircraft may operate at great *speed* acting generally far more quickly than ground- or sea-based vehicles. Aircraft also operate with limitations, notably impermanence. Even today, with the advantages of air-to-air refuelling and very long endurance, no aircraft can remain indefinitely over its objective. An aircraft cannot hold territory nor can it substitute for 'boots on the ground', although that has not stopped military planners from trying to make them do exactly that.

There is no question that aircraft have fundamentally changed the conduct of war on land and at sea at the *tactical* level. However, since aircraft achieved the range to cross enemy lines and strike at an enemy's cities and bases, there has been a strong current of thinking that air power can have *strategic* effect and achieve political goals alone. It is this hope that drives contemporary politicians in many countries to see air power as one possible solution to extremely difficult political or security problems. The argument as to whether aircraft can indeed achieve strategic results runs throughout this book.

Vast resources have been and are spent on the development and production of military aircraft. This continues, now as much as ever. Questions concerning the development, deployment, and potential of air power, whether they like it or not, are everyone's concern; aside from any other consideration, everyone is paying for it.

Since the very beginning it was clear that the new technology would have military applications. The Wright brothers, who made the first powered flight in 1903, were not the homespun bicycle-makers of legend, or rather were not only that. They were very familiar with complex aeronautical mathematics and engineering theory, just as today's aircraft engineers must be. It was clear from the start that aircraft would have a military dimension, and the Wright brothers were explicit that they were looking for military contracts to continue their work, which they eventually received. In 1908, Lord Northcliffe, a British newspaper magnate, sent a telegram: 'aeroplane primarily intended war machine stop'.

The First World War (WW1), which we will examine in Chapter 2, demonstrated that aeroplanes would indeed be war machines, and very formidable ones. Whilst it was never a decisive arm on any WW1 front, all the elements of its future deployment were present with the exception of its potential for mobility. By the end of the war, the combatant nations had thousands of aircraft in their inventories with their attendant administrative and logistical structures. The world's first independent air arm, the Royal Air Force, had been formed. The years after WW1, examined in Chapter 3, saw theorists looking at how this promising new military dimension might be deployed most effectively. These theorists argued that the nature of war itself had now changed, that all elements of a nation might now be in the front line. Air power could win wars alone, they said, either by terrorizing citizens to the extent that they would force their governments to capitulate or through demolishing a state's industrial capability to sustain a war. This was and is termed 'strategic bombing', although there is rarely anything 'strategic' about it. Most importantly, air power offered the possibility that future conflict might be cheaper than the 'old' wars, in both lives and money.

Not all air forces bought into these ideas; the pre-Second World War (WW2) German and Soviet Air Forces saw their roles primarily as supporting the army by attacking the enemy's deployed forces. All of these ideas and many more were put to the test in WW2 and will be dealt with in Chapters 4 and 5. Whole cities were devastated by bombing: Dresden, Hamburg, Hiroshima, Nagasaki, and Tokyo being only the best known amongst dozens of others. Whilst arguments still rage as to the strategic effectiveness and indeed the morality of these operations, there is no dispute that aircraft were vital to battlefield success in the war in both Europe and North Africa. In the Pacific, US industrial power created a large and highly efficient aircraft carrier fleet, with the aircraft and trained crews to man them.

Chapters 6 and 7 deal with the Cold War period after WW2 by examining the 'small wars of peace', many of which were anything but small or peaceful. More bombs were dropped during the Vietnam War than all of WW2, causing great damage but having questionable effect, to say the least, on its political outcome. Other conflicts from South Asia to the Middle East, from Africa to the South Atlantic, saw aircraft as decisive on the battlefield. The end of the Cold War was marked by what appeared to be something of a shift. Some new thinking brought air power once again into play as a possible 'war-winner' in the First Gulf War of 1991 and the Balkan Wars. Even here the truth is more nuanced than air power enthusiasts might wish to believe.

Chapters 8 and 9 bring us into today's world of the wars on 'terror', drones, and cyber-war, and consider briefly what air power may look like in the future.

Like any other field of military activity, air warfare has produced an alphabet soup of acronyms. There is, I am afraid, no real way of avoiding them entirely. Terms are given in full at first usage along with the acronym and subsequently acronym only; there is a complete list of abbreviations at the start of the book. Before embarking on the story of military air power, we will visit an air base near a conflict zone today, where a mission is being prepared to attack a target in enemy territory.

Anatomy of an air strike

Intelligence officers and imagery analysts have pored over images taken from manned reconnaissance aircraft, drones (also known as RPAS ('Remotely Piloted Aircraft Systems') or UAV ('Unmanned Aerial Vehicle'), and satellites. They have selected the target; lawyers have confirmed that hitting it conforms with international humanitarian law, the law of war, and senior officers or even politicians have approved the mission. Engineers have ensured that the aircraft are airworthy, and armourers have placed the correct bombs and missiles (known as 'ordnance') onto the bomb-racks and loaded the guns. Flight operations personnel fuel the aircraft. Fire-crews and medical personnel are on constant stand-by. A 'combat search and rescue' team is briefed; the team will go in by helicopter and 'extract' aircrews who are shot down and eject over enemy territory. All are fed and sustained by a highly complex and usually smoothly functioning administration and logistics system, which itself benefits from the advantages offered by transport aircraft (mobility) which can move supplies or personnel anywhere in the world very quickly.

The crews flying the aircraft in the mission (which is sometimes called a 'strike package') are briefed with the latest imagery and information on the enemy's defences. They enter their cockpits, complete their own checks ensuring the aircraft software is correctly updated and communicating with other elements of the mission. When the time comes for take-off, air traffic control ensures airspace ahead of the strike package is clear. If neutral territory is to be overflown, diplomats may have obtained clearances. Once aloft Aerospace Battle Management (ABM) teams take over and ensure the mission is coordinated with allied forces in the area.

ABM is sometimes based in large aircraft packed with radars and detectors which range the electronic spectrum; as well as surveying the 'battle space' looking for enemy activity they also 'deconflict' with other nations' aircraft which may also be operating in the area.

A 'quick-reaction alert' (QRA) fighter element is on standby to deter curious or indeed hostile attention. There is also likely to be an 'electronic countermeasures' (ECM) aircraft, packed with powerful jamming equipment, in support. The ECM crew will be trying to jam the enemy's radars and disrupt their electronic networks. All the time the strike package is itself using an extensive suite of electronics to detect possible threats. All of these activities are intended to ensure that there is adequate *control of the air* to enable the mission to proceed. ABM will also coordinate any air-to-air refuelling (AAR) that may be required on a long-range mission.

Upon entering the enemy's airspace the strike aircraft will need to avoid enemy air defences, and both fighters and ground-based air defences (GBAD). As for anti-aircraft missiles (surface to air missiles (SAMs)), another strike mission may have been ordered to deal with those and their controlling radars—if ECM has not already managed to neutralize them. This is called 'suppression of enemy air defences' (SEAD). Low-level flying skills can also help with this. Once the aircraft arrive at their objective, the target may be 'marked' with a laser. In some circumstances troops on the ground, probably special forces, will mark the target, or global positioning system (GPS) coordinates may be used to achieve great precision for the strike. Either way, it is imperative that in hitting the target the mission avoids, to the greatest extent possible, civilian casualties, as 'collateral damage' may impair the overall war effort by reducing its legitimacy. The aircraft return to base, with all elements remaining vigilant.

This is not the end for this *attack* mission. Satellites or other aircraft must now do a battle-damage assessment to see if the bombs have done the intended damage. They will also conduct the baleful task of assessing whether there has been collateral damage in the form of civilian deaths. The system then begins again and gears up for another attack.

That was a very simple example of a relatively straightforward mission. The reader will appreciate that there are very many 'moving parts' in such a simple operation, as well as very many acronyms! The reader might consider it worth recalling as we go on to look at the history of air power that many missions were orders of magnitude more complex than this one. Imagine the preparation for a WW2 thousand-bomber raid over Germany in the dark, opposed by a ferociously efficient enemy with fighter aircraft and anti-aircraft guns directed by radar. The technology has improved but the four fundamental *roles* of military aircraft—*control of the air*, *attack*, *reconnaissance*, and *mobility*—remain the same.

The four roles of air power: control of the air

The four roles of air power (Box 1) are interdependent and to an extent they are labels of convenience. Some operations may involve all four roles, and aircraft may undertake more than one role.

Without a significant degree of control of the air, the other three elements are impossible to achieve. It is the key enabler for the other main roles of air power. If a commander cannot be assured of air control, the shape of operations will change greatly. Control of the air is not only gained by other aircraft (e.g. fighters) as GBAD may also be highly effective. 'Offensive counter-air' (OCA) involves attacking an enemy's bases and airborne aircraft; clearly if an aircraft cannot take off, it is of no use. This is an example of how one role, attack, can act to achieve another, control of the air. Possibly the best example of this took place on 5 June 1967 when the Israeli air force destroyed much of the Egyptian air force on the ground in a surprise attack (see Chapter 6); for the rest of the Six Day War, Israeli aircraft ranged relatively freely over the battlefields.

7

Box 1. The four roles of air power

(1) Control of the air: ensuring that it is you, not your enemy, that has the freedom of the air. The ultimate aim is 'air supremacy' which is unchallenged control. 'Air superiority' is next best, where enemy challenge is reduced to a minimum. Control of the air is usually gained with the use of fighters; it can also be challenged by effective ground-based anti-aircraft missiles or guns, or indeed by taking or attacking airfields— an approach termed 'offensive counter-air'.

(2) Intelligence, surveillance, and reconnaissance, finding the enemy and learning as much as you can about them. Very commonly, reconnaissance is carried out by dedicated and specially equipped aircraft and satellites, as well as troops on the ground. The acronym ISTAR is commonly used for this function ('intelligence, surveillance, target acquisition, and reconnaissance').

(3) Attack: otherwise known as bombing. Attack is enabled by control of the air and good intelligence. It is the primary means by which air power is exercised on land or at sea. There are three primary forms: tactical bombing against targets on the battlefield; interdiction 'seals the battlefield' from supplies and reinforcements; strategic bombing is directed against the industrial or civilian base of a country.

(4) Mobility: the ability to use aircraft to transport equipment or people—sometimes termed logistics. This can act as a 'force multiplier' for ground forces whether carried out by helicopters at the battlefield or tactical level, or huge transport aircraft which provide 'strategic lift'. Operations can also be sustained by the use of AAR.

Intelligence, surveillance, and reconnaissance

The oldest function of air power reflects the old military adage that a commander needs to 'see the other side of the hill'. The earliest demonstrations of the potential of aircraft were simple attempts to use balloons to acquire sufficient height to see behind enemy lines. In April of 1794, just eleven years after the Montgolfier brothers had flown the first manned hot air balloon, the French army Aerostatic Corps ('Compagnie d'Aerostiers') was formed—twenty-five soldiers were selected for their expertise in chemistry and other relevant fields; commanded by Captain Jean Marie Joseph Coutelle, they were the world's first air arm. The Chateau de Meudon, near Paris, where their balloons were designed and built, has a good case for being the earliest military aerospace research centre.

In June 1794 at the Battle of Fleurus, pilots of the Corps flew the 'Entreprenant'—a tethered hydrogen balloon (Figure 1). They were able to inform the French commander General Jourdan of the movements of Austrian troops by dropping messages and using semaphore. The battle was a significant victory for the French and established their superiority in the Revolutionary Wars of the period, although the Aerostatic Corps was rarely used again. Coutelle and some of his men accompanied Napoleon's expedition to Egypt in 1798. On 1 August of that year the legendary British Admiral Nelson put an end to their plans when he sank the ships carrying most of their balloons and equipment (one of them was the famous *L'Orient*) along with the rest of the French fleet at the Battle of the Nile. The unit was finally disbanded in 1802 when Coutelle and his team were at last able to return to France. The first years of the American Civil War saw both sides deploy balloons to no decisive effect and they were also seen in the Franco-Prussian War of 1870–1. Since 1914, reconnaissance has usually involved the use of powered aircraft utilizing control of the air to observe the enemy and find targets for attack. Again,

1. 'L'Entreprenant' at the Battle of Fleurus 1794.

this can involve using aircraft on or near the battlefield (tactical) or deep behind enemy lines (strategic). Since the early 1960s satellites have played an ever-increasing role, particularly in providing strategic intelligence. Since the late 1990s many reconnaissance aircraft have been unmanned.

Attack

Attack is the application of explosives or other forms of ordnance from the air against enemy forces or indeed civilians. It too has a long pedigree. On 1 November 1911, 2nd Lieutenant Giulio Gavotti of the Italian army air battalion, based in Libya, took off in his flimsy single-seat aircraft and dropped four grenades on Turkish troops just outside Tripoli. He was the world's first bomber pilot. Exactly 100 years later, North Atlantic Treaty Organization (NATO) bombers soared over the same Tripoli skies. The first raid on a civilian target by a heavier-than-air aircraft was on 16 October 1912 during the First Balkan War when a Bulgarian aircraft flown by Captain Radul Milkov dropped two small bombs on Adrianople (now Edirne). No casualties were reported in either operation.

Attack is often used in the *interdiction* role, denying the enemy resupply or reinforcement. For example, during the Ardennes Campaign of 1944, better known as the Battle of the Bulge, Allied air forces had almost entirely stopped the flow of fuel to German army tank units. If a tank cannot move due to lack of fuel it is essentially useless. In modern terminology this is called a 'mobility kill'.

Reconnaissance and control of the air are often used to enable attack by finding targets and clearing the way for strike aircraft (bombers or their smaller relatives, fighter-bombers). When soldiers call upon aircraft to assist them in battle directly, by attacking other soldiers, this is known as close air support (CAS).

Probably the most ferociously contested controversy in air power theory concerns the war-winning potential of air power. One school believes that air power can have a war-winning effect on its own. At the other extreme there are those who believe that air power has only ever been truly effective in achieving war aims when it is used as an adjunct to fighting forces at the tactical (battlefield) level. Most commentators would agree that the answer depends on which war, or indeed which phase of a given war, one is discussing.

Mobility

The fourth fundamental role of air power, air mobility, is vital too, perhaps now more than ever. In 'expeditionary' conflicts of the kind we have seen in Iraq or Afghanistan, the air supremacy enjoyed by the coalition forces was itself dependent on large aircraft bringing in the supplies necessary to sustain the air bases. Indeed, the helicopters which flew troops around their operational zones—providing 'intra-theatre mobility' and often defending these same soldiers from insurgents—are usually themselves flown into 'theatre' (the operational area) inside very large aircraft.

Today, mobility is the most immediately visible function of air power, from the transport of troops to and indeed around operational theatres as well as evacuation of casualties. One vital aspect of current mobility operations is AAR. Air forces that possess this capability enjoy the advantages of greater reach and operational scope.

Dimensions

As with any other successful dynamic system, military air operations exist within a number of physical and conceptual dimensions. First and foremost is *logistics*. US Marine General Robert H. Barrow famously wrote in 1980 that 'amateurs talk about tactics, but professionals study logistics'. All military endeavours require extremely complicated and extensive supply and support networks and the systems to organize them, and air forces are no exception. For a start, all aircraft of all types need bases, requiring large numbers of personnel to build, run, and secure them. Air bases can also be found at sea, aircraft carriers which are the largest warships ever built. US Navy aircraft carriers displace up to 100,000 tons, are 300 metres long, and cost upwards of $10 bn.

Air bases, both on land and at sea, require vast supplies of fuel and, when at war, weaponry, both of which necessitate a long, fragile, and highly organized supply chain. This is in addition to the 'life-support' which any military base requires in the form of basic requirements such as food and clean water. Bases need to be protected, either by a well-trained guard force or, in the case of aircraft carriers, other warships equipped to ward off or defeat attack from surface or submarine forces. Supply networks are difficult to sustain when under active attack by determined enemies from the air or aggressive cyber forces.

Aeronautical development and technology were vastly accelerated by WW1. From then until arguably the early 1990s the global aviation industry engaged in what historian David Edgerton has called 'military and civil leapfrogging' with developments in one being passed into and contributing to the advances of the other. Most of the time, but not always, military developments led the way. In the 1920s and 1930s there was much private investment in racing aircraft, which eventually gave rise to the innovations allowing high-powered all-metal monoplane fighter aircraft such as the Supermarine Spitfire.

The drive for profitable airliners brought similar advances to bombers. The Second World War, like WW1, brought an exponential increase in investment in technology; the jet engine, invented before WW2 (German and British engineers both claimed it as their invention) was first made operational and even mass-produced (by Germany) during WW2. The need for long-range four-engined bombers during WW2 made long-distance jet airliners with pressurized cabins possible and now commonplace.

In the late 20th century, with the advent of large computer and IT industries with huge investment bases in the 1990s, military technologies once again began to follow *civilian* developments. The single exception to this trend today may be drones, where military technology is usually ahead of contemporary commercial applications.

Aircraft need constant maintenance. For example, the Eurofighter Typhoon used by several European countries requires nine hours of maintenance for each hour of flight. The even more complex American F-22 requires forty-five hours with the F-35 needing over fifty. This in turn implies the need for engineers and technicians usually at least as highly qualified as the pilots who depend on them for their safety. Air forces must recruit from the best available young people to maintain the necessary edge over adversaries. Training must be intensive and realistic. During WW2, research demonstrated that Allied bomber crews were most likely to be shot down in their first ten or the last five missions of (usually) thirty in a 'combat tour'. During the first ten missions, their combat skills were beginning to develop and they were more vulnerable. During the final five, exhaustion was assessed as a major factor. A similar pattern was observed in other conflicts, especially Vietnam. Following Vietnam, the US Air Force instituted the 'Red Flag' series of intensely realistic exercises in 1975. Red Flag offers authentic air combat scenarios supported by dedicated 'aggressor' squadrons trained and prepared to fly using the latest 'enemy' tactics. One of the purposes of this is an attempt to overcome the inexperience in combat situations that affects performance during those crucial first few missions in actual conflicts. Red Flag continues to be a major event in the training schedules of many air forces.

In extended conflicts, such as WW2, attrition of pilots and other aircrew was a major problem. The inability of German and Japanese aircrew training systems to replace their losses at anything like the rate of their adversaries contributed greatly to their defeat. Both countries had planned for a short war and had made little provision for extended conflict. By contrast, the United Kingdom's political leadership made a conscious decision that the highest-qualified and best recruits drafted into the armed services should be directed to the Royal Air Force. Huge efforts and resources were put into training and preparing them for combat and setting up the highly complex systems necessary to accomplish this. In a memorandum to the cabinet on the first anniversary of the declaration of war on 3 September 1940, Churchill wrote: 'The Navy can lose us this war, but only the RAF can win it...the bombers alone provide the means of victory.' Clearly this was a view on priorities taken at a level where strategy and political leadership intersected.

When the bullets begin to fly, the effective deployment of air power relies upon good generalship advising and working closely with political leaders. The interplay between politics and air power has been particularly intimate since WW2 and continues today. Political decisions must be carried out down to the level of the battlefield; this requires effective command and control (C2) arrangements. Bringing together all the elements of air warfare and applying them to a particular task can be a very complex business indeed, since it involves many thousands of moving pieces. Successful air campaigns inevitably have strong and robust C2 systems. For example, the Battle of Britain in 1940 was won by the Royal Air Force at least as much by its C2 network (bringing together the various elements of detection, intelligence, command, and operations) as by its fighter pilots. In today's air forces the term 'C3' is also used, meaning 'command, control, and communications', with 'C4' adding 'computers' to the acronym more recently.

Clearly a commander cannot be expected to know every detail everywhere. One way of getting around this problem is to use 'mission command'. This is a technique where a senior commander makes his intent clear and allows subordinates to achieve that objective in their own way, without close supervision. Obviously this requires a high degree of trust. There are limitations to this. With the high cost of modern equipment, resources (especially aircraft) are often scarce and therefore control may need to be exerted more closely in certain circumstances. Likewise, the role of air power as a (supposedly) strategic tool may necessitate more directive control. Today, decisions about dropping munitions on a specific target are sometimes made at high level due to the risk of collateral damage.

Over the last two decades, with the populations of Western countries highly sensitive to the prospect both of casualties to their own forces and those collateral civilian deaths, the question whether or not to use air power has become a matter of national debate. Both politics and law have to a great degree entered the cockpit. There are still some people, even today, who agree with theorist Giulio Douhet's views that laws restraining and governing the use of air power are 'nothing but international demagogic hypocrisies'. Most practitioners of air power recognize that some law or regulation, however apparently ineffective, is better than none. The need for legal regulation of air power was realized early on, as the potential for balloons to cause damage on the ground became clear. The Hague Conventions of 1899 and 1907 had already banned bombing from the air. Although WW1 demonstrated the ineffectiveness of such strictures, serious efforts were made to tighten up and indeed to enforce legal norms. The Hague Rules for Air Warfare (1923) were the first concerted attempt to limit attack from the air. Notably, they restricted bombing to 'military objectives' the destruction of which would 'constitute a distinct advantage to the belligerent'. As has been regularly pointed out since 1923, the term 'military objective' is decidedly imprecise; in wartime almost anything can be made to fall into that category.

The 1977 Additional Protocols to the Geneva Conventions of 1949 brought the law on targeting up to date. These are based around the four central concepts of international humanitarian law: 'proportionality', 'necessity', 'humanity', and 'distinction' between civilians and combatants. The principle of proportionality dictates that any civilian losses must be proportionate to the military advantage gained. Necessity is closely linked, requiring the commander to ensure that only the force necessary to achieve the objective is used; for example, destroying an entire town to get at a single person may be considered neither necessary nor proportionate. The inclusion of the principle of humanity is an attempt to reduce the suffering in war which is why, for example, incendiary weapons such as napalm are now forbidden. Finally, and most importantly, distinction (sometimes called 'discrimination') means ensuring that as far as possible harm to non-combatants is avoided—a vital factor in retaining public support in democratic countries for possibly controversial operations. It is by reference to these principles that our strike package at the start of the chapter will have been cleared, or not, by air force lawyers.

No one would dispute that aircraft and the dimensions that impact upon their use are central to modern warfare. It is easy to forget that—notwithstanding the French Aerostatic Corps of the 1790s and some desultory military ballooning in the 19th century—aircraft are relatively new to the world of conflict. As we will see in Chapter 2, once powered aircraft had taken to the air in the early 20th century, it did not take long for their potential as a military instrument to be realized.

Chapter 2
Beginnings: the First World War 1914–1918

In 1910, General Ferdinand Foch, who was to go on to command all Allied forces in WW1, stated that 'aviation may be fine as a sport ... but as an instrument of war, it is nothing [*c'est zero*]'. It did not take long for that sceptical view, by no means shared by all senior officers, to be compromised by reality. WW1 vastly accelerated the development of aircraft technology, tactics, and operational thinking.

Aircraft were a relatively rare sight over the battlefields of 1914. By 1918, aircraft were organized by major powers into vast air forces. They were regarded by many as an essential, if not as yet decisive factor on the battlefields themselves; further, they had demonstrated their potential to cause damage far behind the front lines.

Reconnaissance

It was in reconnaissance that the nascent air forces of WW1 found their most vital role. In August 1914, the first month of the war, both France and Britain were staring at the very real prospect of defeat by the German army. French and British forces were outflanked. Paris itself prepared for a siege. The Allied forces, in headlong retreat, did not know the location of General Alexander von Kluck's First Army. On 2 September, Corporal Louis Breguet, formerly an aircraft builder, took off with his observer Lieutenant André Watteau in an AG-4 biplane and found the German force. Their information enabled French and British armies to turn and stop the German advance at what became known as the 'Miracle of the Marne'. Breguet surely has at least a claim to have been the 'saviour of France', a title later co-opted by the former air-sceptic Marshal Foch.

As the Western Front, the main theatre of conflict, settled into trench warfare, the primary means of killing the enemy became artillery. No less than 75 per cent of casualties, and probably more, were directly caused by gun barrages. In order for the artillery guns to be directed they needed precise information on the location of enemy positions, their numbers, and strength.

However, placing reasonably well-trained eyes in the sky above those enemy positions would be useful. Aircraft could see troops massing at key points and these in turn could be shelled by long-range artillery. This was the first use of air interdiction—stopping or hindering the enemy getting to the battlefield. If the aircrew could locate the enemy's own artillery positions, so much the better, as they could themselves be targeted with counter-battery gunfire to hit their guns and kill their crews. By the end of the war many of the basic techniques in use for the rest of the century were well established and functional wireless equipment enabled air-to-ground real-time reporting of artillery accuracy, so that artillery commanders could adjust their aim. Aircrew were able to use radio and Morse code to call artillery strikes upon the locations of enemy units they spotted. Precision photography, as well as the capabilities to interpret and analyse images and glean useful intelligence from them, created a lethal combination of air reconnaissance and accurate artillery.

Air power was also important on the Eastern Front. In addition to artillery spotting, aircraft were used by Russian, German, and to a lesser extent Austro-Hungarian forces, to spot the movements of armies over the vast battlefields of what is now Poland and Ukraine.

In August 1914, Russian generals advancing towards German forces ignored warnings of German movements from their Air Corps. General von Hindenburg's staff did not make the same mistake when German pilots provided accurate information on their enemy. The result was a crushing German victory—the Battle of Tannenberg. In June 1916 Russian aircraft provided an excellent overview of Austro-Hungarian defences prior to the Brusilov Offensive, enabling Russian generals to plan a highly effective attack.

Reconnaissance photographs now provide one of the most valuable resources for historians of the war. For the aircrews involved, this was an uncomfortable high-risk task involving precision flying and almost constant bone-freezing cold combined with fear. The risks for all aircrew in WW1 were very great and life expectancies were low.

Once an aircraft was disabled or burning there was no chance of escape, as parachutes were neither issued nor permitted to aircrews. It was not until 1918 that air forces on all sides began to permit them, and they have been seen as an essential piece of equipment ever since, not least for morale reasons since they offer some hope of survival in the event of critical aircraft damage.

The only airmen for whom parachutes were permitted in WW1 were the crews of tethered hydrogen observation balloons, which floated over the front lines of all sides, spotting the fall of artillery shells. These were always very heavily defended by belts of guns. Nonetheless, they were constantly targeted, not only by enemy artillery but of course by fighters. Spotting from highly inflammable balloons was another occupation with a very limited life-expectancy.

Control of the air

The advantages offered by reconnaissance aircraft with their ability to direct artillery to targets far behind enemy lines were quickly appreciated. Consequently the need to shoot down those 'eyes in the sky' drove the development of the so-called 'fighter' aircraft. At an early stage in the war it became clear that such specialized aircraft were needed if control of the air was to be gained. Fighters now began to conduct operations to shoot down other fighters with the objective of gaining and retaining that essential air superiority.

In the early months of the war, attacking the enemy's reconnaissance aircraft was the task of other similarly designed planes. The first fighters were mostly crewed by a pilot and an observer with a machine gun on a swivel mount. One of these observers was French Corporal Louis Quenault who claims the distinction of being the first man to shoot down an aircraft in air-to-air combat on 5 October 1914.

Clearly it would be more efficient to aim the aircraft instead, allowing for a steadier aim and indeed reducing the crew. Given that wings were at the time too weak to support multiple machine guns, this raised the problem of firing through the propeller. Various solutions were attempted. These ranged from mounting the gun over the propeller, to coating the propellers with wedge-shaped steel plates and firing through them hoping for the best. A true system of synchronization of the gun with the propeller was first mastered by the Dutch engineer Antony Fokker, whose *eindecker* (monoplane) aircraft ruled the skies of late 1915. They were equipped with an interrupter mechanism allowing the machine-gun bullets to pass between the spinning propeller blades.

The 'Fokker Scourge' gave rise to the first great slaughter of British reconnaissance pilots and the fighters trying to protect them.

Soon British and French designers incorporated their own interrupter mechanisms. However, the British Royal Flying Corps remained particularly disadvantaged by a haphazard and incoherent training regime for their aircrew. Their adversaries in the Luftstreitkräfte (the German Air Arm) were usually far better prepared for combat. The German air force approach to control of the air gave rise to some highly original tactical thinking, informed by hard-earned experience. In 1916 the leading German fighter leader and tactician Oswald Boelcke drafted a set of precepts for air-to-air combat; these were fully explained in the form of a booklet given to each German fighter pilot on completion of training. The 'Dicta Boelcke' (Box 2) are still studied by fighter pilots today.

On both sides a large proportion of air-to-air kills were made by aces—men who had shot down five or more opponents. The most famous of them all was Oswald Boelcke's protégé Manfred von Richthofen—the famous 'Red Baron'—with eighty kills. By the same token, most victims of the 'aces' were relative novices; this was a pattern that was to continue in WW2.

For most of the war, British pilots were not as well trained as their German counterparts. This resulted in several defeats in the air. Their chances were not improved by the relentlessly aggressive tactics of the RFC Commander, Brigadier (later Major-General) Hugh Trenchard, designed to keep German reconnaissance aircraft away from British lines.

In the last year of the war good British fighter airframes were married to excellent French Hispano-Suiza engines. This, combined with major improvements in training, resulted for the first time in more German aircraft being shot down than British.

Box 2 The 'Dicta Boelcke': sayings of Oswald Boelcke on air fighting

(1) Be sure you have the advantage before you attack (speed, height, numbers, position); attack out of the sun when you can.

(2) Once you have begun an attack, prosecute it to the end.

(3) Open fire only at close range, and then only when your opponent is square in your sights.

(4) Don't let your opponent out of your sight.

(5) In any type of attack, it is imperative that you approach from behind.

(6) If your opponent dives on you, do not try to evade his attack—turn towards your attacker.

(7) When over enemy lines, always keep in mind your own line of retreat.

(8) When fighting in groups, it is best to attack in groups of four or six; when the mêlée begins, ensure that not too many of your own aircraft go after the same adversary.

Both sides learnt from each other throughout the war in tactical and technological terms; however, it is fair to say that for most of the war aircraft technology was led by German designers, culminating in 1918 with the excellent Fokker D.VII; it was just about matched by the French Nieuport, British Sopwith, and Royal Aircraft Factory SE5a aircraft.

French and British air arms were by this time being reinforced by the US Army Air Service, initially led by Lieutenant-Colonel (as he then was) William 'Billy' Mitchell. By the end of the war throughout the Western Front the combination of overwhelming Allied production rates and an increase in relative quality of training and equipment began to tell—attrition took its toll on the

Luftstreitkräfte. Having said that, albeit outnumbered German pilots remained an effective force until the last day of the war.

Attack

Once you have control of the air and understand what it is that needs to be destroyed on the ground through reconnaissance, there remains the option of destroying targets from the air—usually by bombing. This is the third role of air power—attack. As noted in Chapter 1, this may be divided into three categories: tactical or battlefield bombing, interdiction, and strategic bombing, which has often strongly implied or indeed has unequivocally meant attacking civilians or civilian targets.

By 1916, aviation units were becoming major factors in planning ground operations; this was particularly evident at Verdun, one of the deadliest battles of the war, where detailed plans were made and executed by both the French and German air arms to secure control of the air to ensure that the crucial artillery-spotting role was carried out effectively. In 1917, for the first time German ground-attack aircraft were directed by radio onto their targets, a presage of what is now known as close air support.

The combination of air forces challenging for and exploiting control of the air, ground forces acting under air cover and using aircraft to assist their operations, and artillery and armour (tanks) reached a deadly apotheosis in the German blitzkrieg (lightning war) in the early 1940s. This approach was to a great extent based on the experiments of WW1, particularly in the 'Spring Offensive' of 1918 when the German army came very close to defeating the Allies in the west.

By this time German air–land coordination techniques had been finely developed, although with obvious technical limitations. The British and French were of course developing their own methods. During the triumphant, but immensely costly,

'100 days' campaign which brought Germany to defeat in November 1918, the British and French used similar 'joint operations' tactics. Allied, and especially British infantry, artillery, tanks, and aircraft proved themselves at least as capable as their German opponents of acting together in pursuit of their objectives.

Strategic bombing in WW1

The First World War also saw some effective use of strategic bombing, a term generally used to describe bombing economic or industrial targets; this has often resulted in the bombing of civilians. Ten people were killed when a Zeppelin bombed Antwerp on the night of 23–4 August 1914, the first of many hundreds of thousands of such victims of aerial bombing. The deliberate targeting of civilians continued throughout the war. Zeppelin attacks on Britain started with a raid on Yarmouth in Norfolk in January 1915. The airship crews had little idea where they were, having had to contend with weather systems at altitudes which were poorly understood at the time. Eventually the Zeppelins became more accurate and London was struck, causing international concern but little damage and few casualties, at least compared with what came later.

The Zeppelin raids stopped when losses caused by accidents, as well as the occasional unlucky encounter with British fighters, exceeded the capability of the German army and navy to replace them. At this point, the rather more effective Gotha aircraft, multi-engined, purpose-built bombers based on a Russian design, appeared over London in May 1917 in Operation Turks Cross ('*Turkenkreuz*') (Figure 2). Their campaign, the first Blitz, was highly significant. First, about 700 civilians (from a UK total of 1,400 from all air raids) were killed in a city whose inhabitants had regarded themselves as immune from the war—with the exception of the impertinent but not particularly effective Zeppelin raids.

2. Gotha VII bomber.

Second, and rather more significantly for the history of air power, the raids caused a great deal of political pressure to be directed at a government whose air defence forces were seen as ramshackle and ineffective. This resulted in the commissioning of a study and two consequent reports from the former leader of the South African Boer rebels, General Jan Smuts, who had been invited by Prime Minister Lloyd George to join the war cabinet. Taken together, the Smuts Reports have been described as the 'Magna Carta' of air power history.

The first report published in July 1917 dealt with the setting up of a system of air defence involving unified command and control of visual observers, anti-aircraft guns, and fighter aircraft. The resulting London Air Defence Area, devised in 1916 by Major General E. B. Ashmore, was to function within a larger Air Defence of Great Britain system. This programme constituted the world's first integrated air defence system (IADS) and set the pattern for every similar system in subsequent wars and campaigns. The most notable of these was the 'Dowding System' which played a major part in winning the Battle of Britain in 1940.

The second of General Smuts's reports was equally important. It recommended the amalgamation of the army's RFC and the navy's Royal Naval Air Service. The institutional rivalry between the two services had resulted in duplication and huge inefficiency, which was reason enough for joining the two. There was another purpose behind the recommendation, indeed the main purpose: the report stated that 'the day may not be far off when aerial operations with their devastation of enemy lands and destruction of industrial and populous centres on a vast scale may become the principal operations of war'. To carry out this function, the recommendation was for the foundation of an independent service answerable to the authority of a separate government ministry. Accordingly, the Royal Air Force took shape on 1 April 1918. Its first Chief of Staff was General Hugh Trenchard, the same officer who had urged relentless aggression to his fighter pilots in 1916.

A so-called 'Independent Force' was formed under Trenchard's command with the aim of striking hard at targets within Germany. It began an intensive programme of bombing industrial targets, or at least those that could be found and hit with the technology available at the time. By the end of the war the Inter-Allied Independent Air Force, as it was now called, had been joined by French, Italian (whose Caproni Ca 1s were the first aircraft specifically designed as bombers), and American aircraft. Assessments after the war, including by Trenchard himself, concluded that the force had achieved little.

Air power at sea

Very close to the start of the war, Japanese aircraft were launched from the sea to conduct an attack on an enemy fleet in harbour. The enemy in this case was the German fleet bottled up in the besieged port of Tsingtao (now called Qingdao) in September 1914 and the aircraft were four flimsy Farman seaplanes launched from a converted merchant vessel now adapted as a seaplane carrier.

The 25 lb bombs missed, and no damage was done; nonetheless, this was the first raid on a target from the sea, a technique that the Japanese were to master.

However, during WW1 it was the British who were to develop maritime air power with vigour and innovation. Some of the raids they conducted from the sea were effective, notably the Christmas Day 1914 raid on the German port of Cuxhaven where Zeppelins were based. In 1918, the world's first aircraft carrier, HMS *Furious*, a converted cruiser, launched the most effective of all carrier raids of WW1 on Tondern, destroying several Zeppelins. In 1918, the Royal Navy built its first true 'flat-top' aircraft carrier, HMS *Argus*, and was planning a large-scale raid by torpedo bombers on the main German naval base of Wilhelmshaven when their operation was precluded by the end of the war in November of that year.

It was in the anti-submarine role that aircraft really excelled. Airships provided a real opportunity of seeing German submarines, or U-boats, before they became a threat. U-boats and other submarines of that period (indeed until late WW2) spent most of their time on the surface, usually submerging after being sighted by enemy ships or aircraft. Not only were they then far slower and less effective underwater, but they were also more likely to lose sight of their targets. Only one submarine was sunk by an aircraft in WW1, but many ships were saved from being sunk with this new method of early warning.

Setting the terms of air power

By 1918 aircraft were being increasingly integrated into what is known as 'combined arms warfare', working closely with infantry, artillery, and the new armoured units. Further afield, air power was bringing new options for admirals as well as generals. By the end of the war both land- and sea-based aircraft were being seen as far more than the 'eyes' of the surface units.

With the growth of air power, there necessarily grew a vast organizational, industrial, and logistical infrastructure supporting the new air arms. Clearly, there was no turning back. In essence almost all of the roles and missions of current air forces—with the exception of the extensive use of air mobility—were effectively demonstrated, albeit in a technologically embryonic form.

Instead of being seen as a supporting arm for the other services, air forces were beginning to develop their own separate identities, headquarters, staff, and indeed, to a growing extent, culture. The most obvious example of this was clearly the new Royal Air Force, with a strength by the end of the war of 290,000 (including reserves) men and women, and 22,000 aircraft. German, French, and Italian air arms were now mature organizations in themselves.

Finally, WW1 had made clear that attacking enemy facilities of any kind far behind the lines from the air was a very difficult proposition. Bombers not only had to face fighter aircraft and anti-aircraft guns, but even finding, let alone hitting targets in enemy territory was no easy task. Nonetheless, the idea that large numbers of bombers might achieve very great, perhaps even decisive, results had very much taken root.

Chapter 3
Theory and practice: the interwar years 1919–1939

Entirely new armed forces were now being formed—air forces. They would be of little use if they acted without the shaping influence of coherent theory. Theory provides the basis for *doctrine*—the prescribed methods of warfare which differ from country to country. This chapter will look at the new structures, the ideas which informed them, and technical developments, and how all were brought together in the major conflict between the wars, the Spanish Civil War.

Supplying the structures: independent air forces

At the end of the First World War in late 1918 the RAF, the first independent air force, was by far the most powerful air arm in the world. A year later, over 200,000 of its servicemen had been discharged leaving a rump of 28,000. With a deeply indebted government, all armed forces were faced with the necessity of proving value for money. Trenchard was able to argue to British political leadership under David Lloyd George that not only could the RAF win wars; it could do so cheaply. The use of aircraft to substitute for far more numerous ground forces became known as 'air control' or 'air policing' and was carried out on the 'North West Frontier' (the borders of what is now Afghanistan and Pakistan), Somaliland, Iraq, and Aden. It cost the Treasury a small fraction of full military occupation. The term 'air policing' is still used today, often involving the use of drones, not manned aircraft. Remarkably, it is also carried out in the same areas.

France took a similar approach in its conflicts in Morocco (the Rif War 1923–5) and Syria (the Druze Revolt 1925–7). It was during the Rif War in Morocco that the first air medical evacuation units (now known as MEDEVAC) were formed, using converted bombers to take wounded soldiers from the battlefield to hospitals. The RAF carried out the first ever significant troop movement by air in northern Iraq in 1923 when several hundred soldiers were airlifted to reinforce Mosul against a Turkish threat. The potential of air power to assist in a more humanitarian context was demonstrated in Afghanistan during the winter of 1928–9 during one of the country's regular episodes of civil strife. In the first civilian airlift in history the RAF evacuated the 600-strong European community of Kabul.

Meanwhile, across the Atlantic, Brigadier General 'Billy' Mitchell (1879–1936), who had commanded the US Army Air Service in its early days in France, was putting the case for a strong and independent air force in his own way. In 1919 he publicly stated that bombers now had the range and power to render the navy's much prized and very expensive battleships irrelevant; they could now be destroyed from above. In 1921 this claim was tested when aircraft sank the old German battleship the *Ostfreisland* in an experimental test, albeit one conducted in circumstances very favourable to the aircraft. This, as well as constant complaints about the competence of senior officers, won him few friends in senior naval and military circles and later comments concerning army officers resulted in court martial and the resignation of his commission. Nevertheless, Mitchell remained a relentless advocate for air power, writing *Winged Defense* in 1925.

The US Army Air Service became the US Army Air Corps (USAAC) in 1926 and achieved semi-autonomy within the army with a seat on the army general staff. The USAAC was not yet technically an independent service like their counterparts in the UK or Italy, whose Regia Aeronautica was founded in 1923.

Germany was forbidden any air force whatsoever by the crippling terms of the 1919 Treaty of Versailles. This did not stop them from forming and training a core capability that, when the time came, could provide the seeds of a new air force. For the first decade or so this was done in secret. In exchange for technical know-how and cooperation, in 1924 the USSR agreed to provide training bases for the German air force near Lipetsk in western Russia. In 1933, with the accession of Hitler, all pretence was dropped and the Luftwaffe was formally created, built on the foundations illegally laid in the 1920s.

Providing the ideas

The possession of military aircraft was one matter; how to use them effectively was another. Three thinkers set the terms of air power theory and practice for much of the next fifty years. Historian Harry Ransom pithily summarized their respective roles: 'It may be said that Douhet was the theorist of air power, Mitchell the publicist and catalytic agent and Trenchard the organisational genius.'

General Giulio Douhet (1869–1930; Figure 3) had been writing and thinking about air power since 1912 and clearly realized its potential. In his book *The Command of the Air* (*Il dominio dell'aria*, 1921, with a second edition in 1927) he famously stated that 'to conquer command of the air means victory; to be beaten in the air means defeat'. Douhet had witnessed at first hand the slaughter of tens of thousands of Italian soldiers for very little gain during WW1. He argued that air power might be able to avoid this kind of pointless killing. It offered the option of going directly for the enemy's strategic heart. A new frontier in warfare was now opened, the air itself which unlike the land or the sea covered the entire planet. Now that aircraft could range that new frontier, the

3. Giulio Douhet.

first concern of military planners should be the destruction of enemy air bases using large forces of bombers. We would now term this offensive counter-air (OCA); once the enemy's air force was neutralized, bombers could range freely and attack at will, since Douhet believed that effective defence was impossible against large fleets of aircraft. Once command of the air had been achieved and exploited, armies and navies were subsequently relegated to secondary importance as they were now entirely subject to destruction from above.

Further, the new technology meant that the enemy's civilian population and industrial assets were effectively in the front line. Attacking the 'vital centres' of society would mean that civilian morale and the will to fight would be shattered and governments would be forced to sue for peace; he implied that if air power could bypass a state's armed forces and threaten its people and government directly, it would eliminate the need for the kind of battles seen in WW1. The Prussian military theorist Carl von Clausewitz had argued that the defeat of an enemy necessitated the defeat of his armed forces. Douhet implicitly argued that this was no longer the case.

In the United States, 'Billy' Mitchell's legacy lived on in the new USAAC's Air Corps Tactical School (ACTS) based at Maxwell Air Force Base in Alabama. The ACTS incubated a generation of air leaders who became known as the 'Bomber Mafia' for their advocacy of the primacy of precision bombing. In 1946 it became the Air University and is still the intellectual heart of the US Air Force.

Graduates of the ACTS would dominate US air power thinking and planning in WW2, Korea, and Vietnam. These officers based their thinking, as Mitchell (heavily influenced by Douhet) had, around the need to destroy an enemy's 'key nodes'. These would be choke points in military or industrial construction or supply, not civilian centres of population as Douhet envisaged. Striking these would result in the collapse of the enemy's *capability* to fight. This became known as 'industrial web theory'. Great efforts were made in the 1930s to give the USAAC the ability to strike these targets with the necessary precision, notably through the development of the innovative Norden bombsight with which US bombers were equipped in WW2.

Like Douhet, Hugh Trenchard believed that bombing was the heart and purpose of air power. He believed that the moral effect of bombing would be central to its success. In a report on the activities of the Independent Air Force drafted in 1919 he famously claimed, with no supporting evidence whatsoever, that the moral effect of bombing 'stood to the material effect in a proportion of 20–1'. The report goes on to opine that more damage was caused to German industry by air raid alarms driving workers from their factories than the bombs themselves. Trenchard oversaw the development of the *Royal Air Force War Manual* (also known as AP1300) released in 1928. AP1300 echoed the stress placed by Mitchell and the ACTS and referred to vital centres: 'Objectives should be selected ... which will have the greatest effect in weakening the enemy resistance and his power to continue the war.' Rather than attacking civilians directly, as Douhet advocated, Trenchard's approach was to attack targets which would erode the enemy population's will to fight rather than the enemy's physical *capability* to do so, which was the focus of Mitchell and the ACTS.

So much for the Allies; what of the German intellectual approach to air power? The Luftwaffe was led from the start by Hermann Goering, one of Hitler's oldest political associates. He was a former fighter pilot whose lack of perspective on aspects of air warfare such as supply, logistics, engineering, and doctrine proved seriously damaging. However, the new German air force had some very capable leaders. Its first and most effective Chief of Staff Walther Wever (1887–1936) understood that the Luftwaffe had to complement the army and navy.

Wever drafted *Die Luftkriegführung* (Conduct of the Air War), better known as Regulation 16. This stressed the importance of air power's role in the defeat of the enemy's *field* forces ignoring any grand ideas about air power winning wars on its own. Attacking one's enemy's civilian population was thought to be actively counterproductive, being more likely to increase than reduce its will to resist. The focus for the Luftwaffe in the initial phase all its campaigns was to gain control of the air (in German *Luftüberlegenheit*) with the use of OCA, eliminating the enemy air force as an effective threat by destroying its aircraft and supply networks. Further, whilst Wever took the view that, in his words, 'the decisive weapon of air warfare is the bomber', diverting these assets from their primary role of destroying the enemy's bases and aviation factories was considered wasteful. Wever endeavoured to ensure a balanced force with a focus on 'joint' operations (i.e. close cooperation between the army and air force). Fortunately for the British, amongst others, the force of heavy bombers advocated by Wever was never developed by his somewhat fractious successors. By 1936, when he was killed in an accident, the Luftwaffe was beginning to take shape as a formidable force.

Developing the aircraft

In the decade after WW1, funding was not available on any major scale (except for a short time in the Soviet Union) for such indulgences as military aerospace research. Accordingly bombers—and indeed fighters—were still slow, fabric-covered biplanes with speeds not much greater than their WW1 predecessors. British and indeed French bombers often had a dual use as transports and cargo aircraft for the scattered garrisons of their respective empires.

Meanwhile civil aviation in Europe was growing rapidly. Although it was still beyond the means of most (a London to Paris return cost £8, about four times an average British worker's weekly salary) the new industry was beginning to pay for itself. The German state-funded Lufthansa grew particularly quickly, carrying more people further in the 1920s than all British, French, and Italian airlines put together. Indeed, military planners in interwar Germany regarded Lufthansa as an opportunity to train pilots for the bombers they were forbidden to have, but very much planned to develop.

Until the early 1930s, at least in the democratic West, the technology of civil aviation outstripped that of its military counterparts. Many 1930s passenger aircraft were developed into bombers during the period immediately prior to WW2. *All* transport aircraft used by air forces until the early 1950s were developed from civilian models.

Prior to the mid-1930s it was only in the Soviet Union that serious advances were made in *military* aviation on a significant scale. For example, in 1931 Russian aircraft designers produced the Tupolev TB3, the world's first four-engined monoplane bomber. During the 1930s, the Communist government had encouraged much the same enthusiasm for aviation as seen in the West. Records were set and heroic flights achieved, including the first landing at the North Pole. Millions joined the 'Society for defence and the aviation-chemical industry of the USSR', fortunately abbreviated to Osoaviakhim. By 1941 it had trained many tens of thousands of pilots and engineers for military service.

It was in the Soviet Union that what is now known as airborne warfare—dropping soldiers by parachute into battle—developed on a significant scale. Prior to 1937 the Soviet air force was the largest and certainly one of the most modern in the world. Unfortunately for the USSR, most of its innovative designers and forward-thinking generals were imprisoned or killed during Stalin's purges of the late 1930s, setting the USSR back many years. An emphasis on quantity replaced innovation and quality. In 1941 the USSR was to pay a very heavy price both in the air and on the ground for the loss of some of its best military minds.

Rise of the fighter

In the 1920s and 1930s, however, there was a feeling that, as British Prime Minister Stanley Baldwin had told the House of Commons in 1932, 'the bomber will always get through'. There was a belief, indeed an acceptance, that the civilian population of major cities was now a target and that when the day came, destruction would be absolute.

However, others believed that the bomber would by no means 'always get through'. Billy Mitchell himself had said in 1919 that fighters (or as they were called in the USA at that time 'pursuit' aircraft) were 'the basis on which an air force rests' and retained the view that fighters were an essential component of any air force. No air force had lost the expectation that a powerful defence could be mounted against aerial assault and the fighter had its effective partisans everywhere, notably Clair Chennault at the ACTS in the USA, who would go on to command China's 'Flying Tigers' units in 1941.

In the early 1930s, fighters were not significantly faster than bombers. It was reasonable to assume, as various exercises had proved, that bombers would be very difficult to locate and shoot down. As the decade wore on, much faster and better armed fighters were being developed often as a result of civilian developments in air racing. Britain had the Supermarine Spitfire and Hawker Hurricane—fast, manoeuvrable, all-metal (or in the case of the Hurricane mostly metal) eight-gun interceptors a generation ahead of the fabric-clad biplanes they replaced. Both were a match for the best fighter the Germans could produce, the Messerschmitt Bf 109, first seen in public at the 1936 Berlin Olympics.

Considerable thinking was applied to the problem of air defence, particularly in the UK. This involved a combination of scientific insight, military determination, and supportive political oversight especially from Sir Neville Chamberlain, Prime Minister 1937–40. The most important single figure was Sir Hugh Dowding who took charge of supply and research within the air staff in 1930. Although without technical scientific training he took the time to gain a clear understanding of the technology available at the time. Dowding ensured funding for the most important of these, radio direction finding (RDF), invented by Robert Watson-Watt. In 1936 Dowding became commander-in-chief of the newly created Fighter Command. It was there that he oversaw the system that was to take his name—the Dowding System (see Chapter 4).

Strategic bombing begins in earnest: Spain and China 1936–1939

For all the glamour, fear, argument, and propaganda it had produced, air power had not yet had a decisive, truly strategic role. This changed on 27 July 1936 when the Spanish Moroccan Transport Company was founded with an endowment of 3 million German Reichsmarks. It was given a couple of dozen Junkers 52 transport aircraft and airlifted General Franco's ruthlessly capable Army of Africa from its bases in Spanish Morocco to Spain. This was of course a Luftwaffe operation, codenamed Magic Fire (*Feuerzauber*). It shifted the balance of power in favour of the nationalist rebels and changed Spanish history. So it was that the first use of air power which had real political or strategic effect was an operation carried out by transport aircraft, not bombers.

The Junkers were the vanguard of the Condor Legion, an expeditionary force of volunteers from the newly founded Luftwaffe. After heavy fighting, the Condor Legion, armed with new Messerschmitt Bf 109 fighters, succeeded in wresting control of the air from the almost equally modern Soviet I-15 biplane and

I-16 monoplane fighters sent by Stalin to assist the Spanish Republican forces. The Luftwaffe's new Heinkel 111 bombers and Junkers 87 Stuka dive-bombers fully exploited the freedom gained in conducting interdiction of Republican supplies and reinforcements (Box 3). The Germans were also not averse to bombing cities and civilian targets alongside Italian and Spanish aircraft. A series of raids on Madrid in November 1936 served to confirm to German commanders that bombing of civilians served little purpose. As combat experience was gained, operational doctrine was honed, especially the tricky business of coordination with ground forces which required then as it does now extensive and realistic practice if it is to be effective. The combination of the operational techniques they developed would become known in 1939 as 'blitzkrieg' (lightning war), a term never used in German doctrine.

The Italians had also been involved alongside the Germans in the Spanish Civil War, though less effectively. They had also been engaged in a savage war of conquest in Ethiopia since 1935 and despite the heritage of Douhet had not taken the development of ideas suitable for contemporary warfare particularly seriously.

Meanwhile, on the other side of the world, the third major member of what was to become the Axis alliance was in action. In 1937 Japanese forces invaded China from their illegally acquired and held puppet state of Manchukuo (Manchuria). Raids by the Japanese army air force killed many thousands of civilians in China, notably in May 1939 when as many as 12,000 people were killed in a series of raids on the Chinese city of Chongqing (4,000 more were killed by raids in 1941). These were probably the most devastating air attacks prior to the Allied Combined Bomber Offensive against Germany in WW2. During this period, the Chinese Nationalist Air Force (the Republic of China Air Force), initially with foreign, especially Soviet, assistance, made valiant but futile attempts to resist. Indeed, the first air-to-air battle between all-metal monoplanes took place (Chinese Boeing P26s

Box 3 Guernica: the first 'shock and awe' raid

On 26 April 1937 the small, but nationally significant Basque town of Guernica was attacked by about thirty aircraft of the German Condor Legion led by Wolfram von Richthofen, the cousin of the famous First World War ace. It was probably the first combat mission for the new Messerschmitt Bf 109 fighter. The raid was planned as one of a series with the primary aim of destroying major transport intersections. About 200 civilians were killed and very few soldiers. There had been more casualties in a similar raid on the smaller town of Durango three weeks previously.

Although Guernica is often and understandably seen as an example of terror bombing, German air doctrine did not advocate bombing of civilian targets unless it might produce a direct benefit for ground forces, such as blocking an enemy's retreat. The purpose of this and most such raids was primarily tactical, with a by-product of sowing terror and confusion in Republican ranks, both civilian and military.

What made this raid significant was a combination of vivid, horrified, and credible international media reports, particularly by *Times* reporter George Steer, and less credible nationalist denials of the slaughter. It was the first time that the reported destruction of a town caused international fury. Pablo Picasso produced a striking interpretation of the bombing; 'a cry of outrage and horror amplified by great genius', as art critic Herbert Read called it (Figure 4). A copy of it hangs outside the Security Council chamber at the United Nations in New York (the original is in Madrid's Prado Museum). On 6 February 2003 this reproduction was covered up, allegedly at the behest of the US delegation, prior to Colin Powell's speech advocating the use of force against Iraq. Just over a month later the invasion of Iraq began with several days of 'shock and awe' air bombardment.

4. *Guernica* by Picasso.

vs Japanese Mitsubishi A5Ms) in August 1937. The Sino-Japanese War was characterized by extreme brutality and the loss of millions of lives. It ended only with the dropping of the two atomic bombs in August 1945.

Air power at sea takes shape

Away from the Chinese War the Japanese navy was developing its own air power and the means to project it. Inspired by the British Royal Navy example in WW1 and assisted initially at least by British advisers, they began to develop the world's strongest force of aircraft carriers, maritime aircraft, and excellent sailors and airmen. By 1941, as events were to prove, they were the only navy in the world capable of launching large air operations from multiple aircraft carriers—a skill their American opponents quickly mastered. However, Japanese training and development regimes incubated serious weaknesses, which whilst not initially fatal, were to be seriously damaging—notably the failure to set up an extensive regime for the training of replacements for their first-rate naval aircrew. The fact that the army and navy had entirely different inventories of aircraft caused unnecessary duplication in an industrial culture that had none of the vast expansive potential of the USA.

Like the Japanese, the US Navy had made great strides in naval air power, moving well beyond its role as the initially envisaged 'eyes of the fleet'. The first carrier, the USS *Langley* (a converted collier), entered service in 1922. A series of legendary carriers followed in the 1930s, including the three Yorktown class ships (USS *Yorktown*, USS *Saratoga*, and USS *Lexington*) which held the line in the early days of WW2. Much thought had gone into how this new capability might be used to support offensive roles such as landings from the sea (amphibious operations) alongside an extensive US Marine Corps Air Arm, as well as fighter tactics to help defend the fleet.

The pioneers of maritime air power in WW1, the Royal Navy, languished in the interwar years. With the Washington Naval Conference of 1921 limiting new tonnage, the Royal Navy had to make do with their WW1 ships. Even more damagingly, the perennial interservice squabbling had given the navy's air arm to the Royal Air Force, who, to put it mildly, did not see it as a priority. Consequently, although the Fleet Air Arm was returned to the Royal Navy in 1939 and new carriers were built, their aircraft were a generation out of date. Events in WW2 were to prove, however, that whilst its equipment was out of date, the Royal Navy had retained its aggressive and innovative edge.

Many of the military capabilities that had evolved during WW1 were developed and improved during the interwar years, different nations building on individual strengths. Germany built on their traditions of land warfare to produce the Luftwaffe, which was designed and built primarily to support the army. Japan, with its freshly minted naval tradition, focused on aircraft carrier tactics and operational matters. In Britain, escalating concerns about the threats supposedly posed by fleets of bombers drove the imperative of building an adequate defence in an attempt to ensure that those bombers would not get through. This took the form of new technologies such as radar and effective fighters, and incorporating them into a formidable system. Similarly, in both the UK and USA, heavy bombers were seen as a means of providing both a forward defence and a deterrent.

Chapter 4
The Second World War: air operations in the West

Air power on the battlefield 1939–45

The Second World War began in September 1939 when Poland was faced with two invasions: the first Nazi blitzkrieg from the west and Soviet armies in collusion with Germany attacking from the east. The Polish air force lasted three days as a reasonably effective fighting force under a well-planned assault from the Luftwaffe. The Poles were greatly outnumbered and hamstrung by a lack of up-to-date fighters and the systems necessary to control them.

When the time came to invade France in May 1940 the Germans had produced a highly efficient organization. Luftwaffe and army commanders were placed alongside each other; they received all the information from both ground and air units, including air reconnaissance. This allowed centralized allocation of resources to support ground troops based upon the best available information, thereby avoiding limited resources being used in a piecemeal fashion.

The German 'operational air war' was rendered even more effective as the Germans deployed their air power in semi-independent 'air fleets' (*Luftflotten*), composed of bombers, fighters, transport, and reconnaissance units which could be moved within operational theatres or indeed between them.

During the invasion of the USSR in June 1941, the Germans adapted and implemented their operational air war on a vast scale. Excellent C3 structures along with a strong emphasis on reconnaissance caused havoc for Soviet forces. The Luftwaffe began the campaign, Operation Barbarossa, in June 1941 with a series of attacks that destroyed much of the Soviet air force on the ground (a technique repeated by the Israelis in 1967). However, it took less than two years for Soviet air forces to be reorganized, assisted by the relocation of factories east into the Urals and further, far beyond the range of potential German air attack.

Fleets of fighters, bombers, and especially regiments of formidable, heavily armed and indeed armoured CAS aircraft such as the Ilyushin Il 2 Sturmovik were formed into 'air armies'. Air armies were almost always attached to Soviet army groups. The tables were turned as the Soviet high command could now apply support on a vast scale where it was required. They were helped by the fact that Allied bombing of Germany had drawn much of the Nazi fighter force back home, leaving the Soviets with a much-depleted Luftwaffe force challenging for control of the skies.

It was in the Mediterranean theatre of operations, where Air Chief Marshal Sir Arthur Tedder commanded the RAF's Middle East Command, that the Western Allies began to learn how air power could be directed on the battlefield itself. Tedder and his team, notably his immediate subordinate, Air Marshal Arthur Coningham, who commanded the Desert Air Force, were not too proud to learn from their enemies. Several of their approaches were derived from Luftwaffe blitzkrieg operational techniques and indeed from British interwar thinking. These techniques included co-locating air and land force headquarters near to the front line, and simplified and efficient C2 arrangements to ensure that air support got to the right place at the right time in the right quantity. Very close cooperation between intelligence and operational officers was also considered vital.

The RAF's hard-learned lessons concerning C2 were largely adopted by the US Army Air Forces (renamed from US Army Air Corps in 1941). They were encapsulated in the seminal US air doctrine document FM 100–20 of 1943 which provided the basis for US thinking on air–ground cooperation for several decades. Its striking opening words are printed in bold capitals: 'LAND POWER AND AIR POWER ARE CO-EQUAL AND INDEPENDENT FORCES; NEITHER IS AN AUXILIARY OF THE OTHER.'

FM 100-20 stated that the three priorities of the application of air power were control of the air, interdiction, and finally CAS. By December 1942, with control of the air over North Africa secured, British and Allied forces were pursuing, harassing, and interdicting the German and Italian armies who were in headlong retreat in North Africa. Meanwhile, squadrons of torpedo bombers sank thousands of tons of shipping in the Mediterranean, causing very great problems for German and Italian supply lines. These interdiction operations were vital to the British victory at the Battle of El Alamein in October 1942 and in subsequent Allied operations to clear German and Italian forces from North Africa.

Excellent inter-service cooperation, and the techniques developed in North Africa and later in Sicily, produced devastating results when the Allies invaded north-west Europe in mid-1944. By then air superiority had been gained and Allied tactical air forces ranged freely over German armies causing mayhem; further, the 'fighter-bomber' had evolved. Aircraft such as the British Hawker Typhoon or the American Republic P47 Thunderbolt were able to attack ground targets with rockets or bombs and deal on even terms with enemy fighters. Luftwaffe fighters were a rare sight over France. The Allies did to the German army what the Germans had done to the Poles and French in the early days of the war. The techniques and procedures for CAS developed in the later years of WW2 are still used today, but require constant practice to be effective.

Securing control of the air: the Battle of Britain 1940

This time the Luftwaffe would be acting alone as a strategic force, whilst lacking a heavy bombing force or the doctrine to use it. However, by the summer of 1940, the Luftwaffe, which had taken significant casualties already during the campaign to defeat France, was confident that Britain could be forced by them to capitulate. It was a fair bet that the Royal Navy, the world's most powerful, would annihilate any attempt by German armies to cross the Channel—unless the Luftwaffe could challenge it. The purpose of the forthcoming German air assault was primarily to acquire control of the air by destroying the RAF's Fighter Command. Only then might Britain be coerced into a settlement.

The fact that Fighter Command had excellent equipment in the shape of its Spitfire and Hurricane fighters was only part of the story; so did the Luftwaffe with their fast bombers and superlative Messerschmitt Bf 109 fighters. The key to British success was that their air force was part of the Dowding System (the first true integrated air defence system (IADS)), giving the British the ability to see, control, and influence what was happening using maximum economy of force. The British already had some experience with IADS with the development of the London Air Defence Area during WW1.

Early warning was provided by radio-direction finding (RDF) (it became known by its American name 'radar' in 1942); if that failed or was damaged, or after aircraft had crossed the coast when early RDF could no longer detect them, a network of human watchers, the Observer Corps, would track incoming aircraft. All elements would send their information to a central control room which would assess the threat and direct the response. The entire system created what would now be called a 'recognized air picture' (RAP).

In the event that the primary control centre failed or was hit and damaged, information would be routed to reserve control rooms. All this was done over a highly secure network of deeply buried cables. Batteries of anti-aircraft guns protected potential targets. In other words, there was an element of redundancy at every level. Stephen Bungay, author of *The Most Dangerous Enemy* (2000), called it 'a system for managing chaos'. In his *War Memoirs* Churchill wrote that 'All the ascendancy of the Hurricanes and Spitfires would have been fruitless but for this system which had been devised and built before the war.' It took the Germans until 1943 to develop something comparable, and the Japanese never did, to their very great cost, as US bombers obliterated city after city in 1945.

Also vital to the British was a superb supply and repair organization alongside an aircraft industry building two fighters for every one the Germans were constructing—this ensured that at no point did Fighter Command suffer from a shortage of airframes. Further, intense training of ground crew ensured that Fighter Command were able to fly more missions than the Germans could manage. A high number of aircraft is irrelevant if they only fly (or 'generate') a low number of missions or 'sorties'. Clearly this was helped by the fact that the RAF was flying over its own territory.

All of these factors speak of a deep preparedness on the part of the British. No such foresight was present on the German side, which had largely planned on the basis of a quick war. Further, the British had excellent leadership in the shape of Sir Hugh Dowding himself and subordinate commanders such as Keith Park, and good intelligence, logistics, and command and control. Meanwhile, Luftwaffe intelligence constantly underestimated the British ability to regenerate its force.

There is a common view that the Battle of Britain was a victory of the few against the many; a relentlessly efficient, professional war machine brought down by British pluck and determined bloody-mindedness. The truth is the reverse. Professional ruthlessness and efficient organization were more displayed on the British side than the German. As for being outnumbered, there were roughly the same number of British fighters as German ones at the start of the Battle and more at the end.

Above all, the British were very clear about their objectives. It was Fighter Command's task to ensure that Germany did not gain control of the air over the UK. Informed by confusing strategic guidance from senior commanders, German objectives changed. Just as sustained attacks on RAF stations were bearing fruit, with Fighter Command coming under severe pressure over southern England, the Luftwaffe shifted to attacking London, thereby allowing Fighter Command's bases time to recover and an opportunity to take advantage of German weaknesses, notably the very limited range of their Messerschmitt Bf109 fighter escorts. Adolph Galland, who was to become commander of the Luftwaffe fighter force in 1941, described the decision to focus on bombing London as 'perhaps the greatest mistake Goering would make during the war'.

None of this in any way diminishes the British achievement in combat. On the contrary, the Battle of Britain is an object lesson for air power practitioners that extempore solutions—however well applied—are rarely a substitute for profound thought, rigorous preparation, and strategic clarity. That said, the Battle of Britain was as much won by the many maintainers, aircraft fitters, RDF plotters, and other less glamorous roles as by the RAF's 'Few' fighter aircrew.

In conceptual terms the battle demonstrated that a *defensive* air campaign could have strategic and political effect. The Battle of Britain secured Britain's place as a key combatant. It also asked serious questions about whether daytime bombing was a sustainable activity.

'Reaping the whirlwind': the bomber offensives 1942–1945

The Luftwaffe offensive against Britain's cities after the Battle of Britain itself, conducted largely by night and ending in May 1941, cost the lives of 43,000 people (thousands more were killed later in the war by bombing, V1 cruise missiles, and V2 rockets). The *primary* purpose of Luftwaffe bombing of London and other cities during the Battle of Britain was not to kill civilians, but to damage industrial capacity—civilian dead being an acceptable but not deliberate by-product. From the British perspective this was an academic distinction, and the effects of the Blitz provided ample political impetus for the more lethal bomber offensive of the RAF. It was now that the elaborate theories of Douhet, Trenchard, and Mitchell were to be put to the test.

The first two years of RAF Bomber Command operations achieved very little. The first operations were conducted in daylight against military or vital industrial targets. The misapprehension that unescorted, lightly armed bombers could survive and operate in the presence of effective fighters over hostile enemy territory in daylight was soon viciously disproved. Unescorted bombers were highly vulnerable, a lesson the USAAF was to relearn.

The British, by necessity, then bombed only at night. The three skills that the RAF would need for this—night flying, bomb-aiming, and navigation—had been neglected by the air staff before the war. Even finding targets, let alone hitting them, was impossible without adequate technology. A senior civil servant, David Butt, was commissioned to examine how successful the first year of raids had been. In August 1941 he and his team reported that—even in good weather and visibility—only one bomber in three dropped its bombs within five miles (8 km) of the target. Precision was going to be difficult if not impossible to achieve at night.

Air Chief Marshal Sir Arthur Harris took over Bomber Command in February 1942. As he said shortly after taking up the post, the Germans 'have sowed the wind, now they will reap the whirlwind'. Harris was never an advocate of purely morale (or 'terror') bombing, but strongly believed that the only way to defeat Germany was to smash its industry, even if that meant killing large numbers of civilians since Germany's industrial might lay in its cities. It is important to stress that Harris did not set policy. As an *operational* commander, his role was not to make policy, but to execute it.

In early 1942, Germany and its allies had the upper hand in every theatre. The bomber offensive was now the only way to strike back at Germany. It was to be the 'main effort' of British military and industrial might. The Area Bombing Directive of 14 February 1942 authorized Harris to 'employ your forces without restriction'. The primary objective was to be 'the morale of the enemy civil population and particularly the industrial workers'.

Technology improves

The RAF still faced the extremely tricky problem of finding and hitting their targets. Radio and ground-scanning radar (such as 'Gee' and 'H2S' respectively) navigation aids were developed for the RAF's new four-engined heavy bombers, particularly the excellent Avro Lancasters which vastly strengthened the British force from 1942 onwards. Squadrons of specialist 'Pathfinder' crews, often flown in the superlative Mosquito aircraft constructed largely of plywood and equipped with the 'Oboe' beam tracking system, were set up by Bomber Command. Their role was to find the targets and guide the bombers onto them using flares and radio. At night it was rare to be able to hit a specific target. Consequently, for most of the war RAF Bomber Command engaged in 'area' bombing. The result of this was vast numbers of civilian dead as a by-product of 'dehousing' industrial workers, one of Harris's objectives, and destroying their factories.

The battle between the rapidly developing German IADS, especially flak guns and radar-equipped night fighters, and British night bombers ebbed and flowed. Hamburg was subject to a particularly shattering attack in July–August 1943 appropriately codenamed Operation Gomorrah. Fire storms killed at least 35,000 and destroyed three-quarters of the city, shaking the Nazi regime. Although many, indeed most, German cities were seriously damaged, the levels of casualties inflicted in Operation Gomorrah were not repeated with a large city until similar raids burnt Dresden (Operation Thunderclap) in February 1945 with over 30,000 killed—a joint operation with the US Eighth Air Force. Bomber Command sustained very high casualties in its campaign against Berlin during the winter of 1943–4. Some RAF raids, such as that on Nuremburg on 30 March 1944, sustained a loss-rate of 11 per cent. With crews expected to fly thirty missions this was unsustainable—few would survive such odds over time. Most raids sustained 3–4 per cent losses.

However, as navigation and bomb-aiming capabilities grew, RAF bombers conducted some impressive precision raids, most famously the 'Dambusters' raid (Operation Chastise, May 1943) and sinking the battleship *Tirpitz* in Norway (Operation Catechism, November 1944). For the last two years of the war, as the British bombed at night, the US Army Air Force was fighting its way across occupied Europe and Germany itself—by day.

The bomber offensive becomes 'combined'

The USAAF had arrived in some force in the UK by late 1942 and the ensuing year saw them build their bomber forces in England as the Eighth Air Force. Armed primarily with B17 Flying Fortress bombers equipped with the Norden bombsight, the Eighth had arrived in the UK with a pre-prepared list of 177 targets, a plan devised by graduates of the Air Corps Tactical School. It was known as AWPD-42 (for air warfare plans division 1942) and although more of a guideline than an operational plan, its objective was to put Germany out of the war in six months.

In the summer of 1943 they put their 'industrial web theory' of precision daylight bombing of selected industrial sectors (in this case ball-bearings and fighter engines) to the test. As the RAF had already discovered, and warned, daylight bombing was a doomed endeavour without strong fighter escorts. Further, the degree of precision that could be attained over training areas in the deserts of Arizona was impossible in the swirling weather of northern Europe with the added elements of attack by a brutal combination of fighters and anti-aircraft artillery (known as 'flak'). The first major raids on Schweinfurt and Regensburg were failures, with up to 30 per cent casualties. The German IADS worked well and the bombers were cut down by a capable German day-fighter force, supported by an efficient radar system. For both the RAF and USAAF the winter of 1943–4 was a crisis point in the campaign.

With the Allied invasion of France approaching, a clear shift in strategy applying to both air forces had already been foreshadowed by Allied senior leaders at Casablanca in January 1943. The two bomber offensives were now to become the 'Combined Bomber Offensive'. Their initial objective was to prevent supplies and reinforcements reaching German forces opposing the Western Allies' invasion of France—this was interdiction at the strategic level. It was known as the 'transportation plan' (March–August 1944) and involved the destruction of railways, bridges, and roads in France. Much of this task would be accomplished by the Allied Tactical Air Forces, RAF and USAAF formations largely armed with twin-engined fast bombers and formidable fighter-bombers such as the American P47 Thunderbolt and the rocket-armed British Hawker Typhoon.

To achieve this implied gaining control of the air. The Casablanca Directive treated this as a priority—specifically the requirement 'to impose heavy losses' on German fighters. The Pointblank Directive of June 1943 supplemented Casablanca and instructed Allied strategic air forces, specifically the Eighth Air Force, to destroy the industries supporting the Luftwaffe. By late 1943 the Americans had the tools to achieve this, the most important of which was a fleet of excellent long-range fighters such as the P47 Thunderbolt, the P38 Lightning, and most formidable of all, the P51 Mustang. The P51 was a fighter with superb flying characteristics (it was nicknamed 'the Cadillac of the skies') and, most importantly, fitted with new drop-tanks it had the range to escort bombers to Berlin itself—and back (Figure 5).

From January 1944 onwards, General 'Jimmy' Doolittle took over command of the US Eighth Air Force. He was already legendary

5. **Flight of P-51 Mustang fighters.**

for his raid on Tokyo in April 1942 (see Chapter 5). Doolittle instructed his highly trained and very well-equipped fighter force to treat escorting the bombers as a secondary task. The bombers themselves would shatter German aircraft factories and fuel supplies. 'The first duty of Eighth Air Force fighters is to destroy German fighters.' This was explicitly to be a battle of attrition and it worked. In the early months of 1944, a particularly intense period, the Luftwaffe fighter force was taking up to 50 per cent losses of aircraft and 25 per cent losses of pilots *per month*. In addition, production of aviation and other fuels was devastated and German forces were compelled to rely on reserves which were quickly depleted. As the relentless attacks wore down Luftwaffe strength, US factories poured out well-designed and constructed fighter and bomber aircraft, and training schools produced excellent aircrew.

There was a certain amount of rancour between Allied commanders as to targeting. In April 1944 General Eisenhower, commanding all Allied forces in Europe, ordered Air Chief Marshal Harris to support the D-Day invasions by attacking German supply lines. He did so reluctantly to say the least, believing it—and indeed D-Day itself—to be a distraction from the main effort. RAF Bomber Command continued the onslaught on cities and towns by night and later in the war by day. Operations over Germany left Allied air forces with effective control of the skies, although an ever-more effective flak force continued to cause serious casualties. Indeed, flak caused nearly 50 per cent of all Allied bomber losses. On D-Day itself on 6 June 1944, 12,000 US and British aircraft were involved, whilst the Germans could put up fewer than 300. In early 1945 Adolph Galland, the commander of Germany's fighter forces, said that 'the danger of a collapse of our Luftwaffe exists'. A series of poor decisions by Goering and Hitler did not help. For example, Hitler ordered the new Messerschmitt 262 jets to be used as bombers, rather than fighters. These aircraft were far superior to anything the Allies possessed and might, if used intelligently, have had a significant—though not decisive—effect on Allied control of the air. By January 1945 British and American bombers were ranging over Europe virtually unchallenged. In the last full year of the war, more explosives were dropped on Germany than in all previous years combined.

It should not be forgotten that occupied countries suffered greatly from Allied bombing campaigns too, experiencing a great deal of what is now called collateral damage. Several French Atlantic ports were devastated by bombers ordered to strike U-boat bases; the latter were never seriously damaged. Indeed France suffered nearly as many civilian deaths (53,000) from Allied air bombing as Britain did from the Luftwaffe during WW2 (60,000). Italian cities were also not spared: 7,000 were killed in Rome and nearly 3,000 in Bologna with many more elsewhere.

The bombing war in Europe: results and controversy

RAF bomber crews sustained the highest casualty rate of any major Allied force. Out of a trained force of 126,000 personnel, 55,573 were killed and over 18,000 injured or captured. A similar scale of losses was sustained by US crews (26,000 in the Eighth Air Force alone, with over 30,000 more killed in the other US air forces deployed in Europe). The morality of the effort is a complex matter and need not be rehearsed in detail here. The arguments involve complex ethical issues of proportionality, necessity, and indeed sometimes the anachronistic application of today's ethical standards to those of the 1940s. Suffice it to say here that at least 380,000 German civilians were killed in often horrible circumstances.

The extent to which this relentless campaign advanced the war effort has been the subject of ferocious and sometimes acrimonious debate ever since. The US Strategic Bombing Survey (USSBS), an extraordinarily extensive account of the effects of the bombing completed in late 1945, concluded that results of the offensive were largely successful, noting particularly its 'catastrophic' effects on oil production. It made the observation that with hindsight air power could 'have been used differently or better in some respects'.

With regard to German industry overall, production of most major assets continued to rise until late 1944, but at far less a rate than would have been the case had the bomber offensive not taken place. There is no doubt whatsoever that by the end of 1944 German military industry (which remarkably only went to a wartime footing in 1943), and the power and transport infrastructure supporting it, was devastated. Even so there was no collapse of morale or society—indeed, solidarity with and dependence on the government both rose. The British Bombing Survey Unit, the British counterpart to the USSBS, reported after WW2 that 'insofar as the offensive against German towns was designed to break the morale of the German civilian population, it clearly failed'.

On the other hand, fully one-third of German artillery, especially the fearsome 88 mm guns which were also lethally effective anti-tank weapons, was engaged in defending German airspace. Twenty per cent of *all* Nazi ammunition was directed into German skies at British and American aircraft, instead of at Soviet, British, or American tanks or soldiers. Instead of fighting at the front or working in factories, 900,000 men were serving those guns. Perhaps most significantly, by October 1944, 80 per cent of German day and night fighters were challenging the bombers rather than vying for command of the air over the Eastern Front, leaving German ground forces to deal with ever more confident Soviet air power more or less on their own. No less than two-thirds of German fighter losses occurred over Germany itself.

Air power at sea

However, without command of the sea routes the USA could not bring its huge industrial resources to bear in Europe or indeed in the Mediterranean where the British were heavily engaged. Securing that lifeline meant defeating the German submarine threat. From the very first day of the war German U-boats (the German word for submarine is *unterseeboot*) attacked British and Allied shipping. As Churchill said in the final volume of his *Second World War*, 'The Battle of the Atlantic was the dominating factor all through the war. Never for one moment could we forget that everything happening elsewhere, on land, at sea or in the air depended ultimately on its outcome.' Air power played a vital role in the defeat of the submarine threat.

Until Germany took France, U-boats had to traverse the North Sea and pass the British Isles, facing attack from the Royal Navy, which limited their endurance in the Atlantic. However, when France fell German possession of its Atlantic ports allowed the U-boats to range further into the ocean and stay longer on patrol there. Bombing these ports succeeded only in killing large numbers of French civilians and destroying their cities. Until mid-1942, helped by a small fleet of German long-range reconnaissance bombers (the four-engined Focke-Wulf Condors), the U-boats wreaked havoc. Monthly totals of tonnage sunk reached catastrophic and unsustainable levels. Without adequate intelligence or long-range surveillance best supplied by aircraft, finding and sinking U-boats was a very difficult task. Three crucial factors cohered in May 1943. First, the British, Canadian, and US navies perfected convoying tactics; second, British codebreaking at Bletchley Park (codenamed 'Ultra') revealed the rough locations of U-boat packs enabling convoys to be redirected away from them; third, long-range aircraft equipped to destroy U-boats became available.

After much debate with Bomber Command and particularly its commander Arthur Harris, who wanted every four-engined bomber directed to the attack on Germany, long-range aircraft with the capability of hunting U-boats were assigned to convoy protection duties. The most numerous of these were B24

Liberators flying out of Northern Ireland. Liberators and Short Sunderland Flying Boats were equipped with radar and depth charges to enable them to locate and destroy U-boats before they got near the convoys. At the very least being spotted by an aircraft would force U-boats to submerge and dive deep to avoid being sunk, thereby breaking contact with their targets. Later, in 1943, convoys could also expect their own air power in the form of small aircraft carriers specially designed for the purpose—escort carriers. No convoy with such a carrier was ever successfully attacked. Also, along the North American coast, the US Navy successfully operated a fleet of powered airships, known as 'blimps', to guard convoys as they entered or left US waters.

The lifeline was secured. By the end of the Battle of the Atlantic, aircraft had sunk about half of the German submarines lost in the Atlantic, with the rest sunk by Royal Navy, Canadian, and US anti-submarine vessels.

These measures allowed supplies to flow not only to Britain, but directly to the battlefields of the Mediterranean. In 1940, the greatest threat faced there was from the formidable Italian navy. As if to prove they had lost nothing of their traditional élan, on 11 November 1940 the Royal Navy's Fleet Air Arm launched a remarkably audacious raid from the aircraft carrier HMS *Illustrious* on the main Italian base at Taranto. The obsolete Fairey Swordfish biplane torpedo bombers succeeded in sinking or disabling three of Italy's powerful battleships, tipping the naval balance in the region decisively towards the British. The raid provided the inspiration for an even more significant encounter at Pearl Harbor just over a year later. The ensuing maritime and air operations in the Pacific were truly epic in scale and we turn to look at them now.

Chapter 5
The Second World War: the air war in the Pacific

On 7 December 1941, Japan's extensive naval preparations, which included a study of the Royal Navy's attack on Taranto, finally bore fruit. Or so it seemed. A fleet of 400 aircraft, flown by a highly trained elite corps of naval aircrew launched from four aircraft carriers, sank six US battleships at anchor in their Pearl Harbor base. At that stage in the war, only Japan was capable of coordinating an attack from multiple aircraft carriers, a difficult and complex task. Unfortunately for the Japanese, the key target, three fleet aircraft carriers (USS *Lexington*, USS *Saratoga*, and USS *Enterprise*), were on exercises at sea.

By way of retaliation for Pearl Harbor, US forces executed a swashbuckling response. On 18 April sixteen twin-engined B-25 Mitchell bombers, under the command of Colonel Jimmy Doolittle, were launched from the aircraft carrier USS *Hornet* stationed 650 miles off the east coast of Japan. The aircraft made their way to several cities at low level, dropped some bombs and flew on to China (one aircraft landed in the Soviet Union) where most of the aircrew were captured. Due to the distances involved it was not possible for the aircraft to return to their carrier base; indeed, recovery to the ship of such relatively large aircraft would have been impossible anyway. The message the raid sent was clear and unequivocal; the Japanese islands were not safe. The raid was deeply shocking for Japanese commanders and a great propaganda coup for the Americans. Remarkably, although most were captured, seventy-one of the eighty aircrew on board the B-25s survived the war.

In early 1942, a series of Japanese successes captured extensive territory in the west and south Pacific. The Malayan Peninsula was overrun, two British battleships were sunk at sea by aircraft, and then the great fortress of Singapore itself was taken in February 1942, arguably the greatest defeat in British military history. The British imperial colony of Burma was taken by May of 1942, and India itself was threatened. Japanese forces swept away US possessions in the Philippines and invaded New Guinea. At one point Australia itself seemed to be at risk of invasion, and indeed the city of Darwin was bombed in February 1942. US forces recovered quickly. At the Battle of the Coral Sea (May 1942), US Navy aircraft sank one Japanese carrier and seriously damaged another for the loss of one of their own. Because the attacks were delivered entirely from the air this was the first ever battle at sea in which neither fleet saw the other.

The first full-scale clash of carrier fleets, the Battle of Midway (June 1942), was a disaster for Japan. The intention was to take the Midway Island group and extend Japan's defensive perimeter, an attractive idea after James Doolittle's raid. Four of their superb fleet carriers were sunk against one American equivalent, the USS *Yorktown*. Whilst Japan could ill afford the loss of so many ships, of equal importance was the loss of so many trained and experienced aircrew. Japanese strategy vis-à-vis the USA was predicated upon a quick war, with the Americans pinned back to their continental homeland. This strategy failed at Midway.

The Japanese lack of any adequate system of training of aircrew as well as their failure to develop new aircraft was ill advised in itself. When taken against the immense industrial and development might of the USA. it was this that the architect of Pearl Harbor, Admiral Yamamoto, who had lived for some time in the USA, truly feared. He had warned against 'waking a sleeping tiger'. Consequently the Japanese were unable to replace losses and were subject to the same laws of attrition which had destroyed the Luftwaffe over Europe.

Yamamoto was killed in April 1943, shot down by US P-38 Lightning long-range fighters. Codebreakers had identified the timing and route of an inspection trip the admiral was making to the Solomon Islands; the fighters struck just before he arrived over the island of Bougainville. This was Operation Vengeance, and it was a good example of the use of air power to achieve strategic effect.

'Island hopping'

The USA was in a position to roll on to the offensive by late 1942 and adopted a two-pronged 'island-hopping' strategy. The central idea of US planners was to bypass very heavily defended Japanese bases and focus on islands that could be taken and used. One thrust, led by General MacArthur, had as its objective the recovery of the Philippines and a move towards South-East Asia and the Japanese mainland itself (this is indicated by line 'A' on the map at Figure 6). It began with slogging battles fought mostly by US and Australian ground forces to retake New Guinea and the Solomon Islands.

The second arm of the strategy (line 'B' on Figure 6), led by Admiral Nimitz, was aimed at establishing bases in the Central Pacific as launch pads for air attacks and an eventual direct assault on Japan from them. This required capturing key islands in the Marshall, Gilbert, and Marianas Island chains. All of these campaigns relied upon Allied air forces taking and securing control of the air.

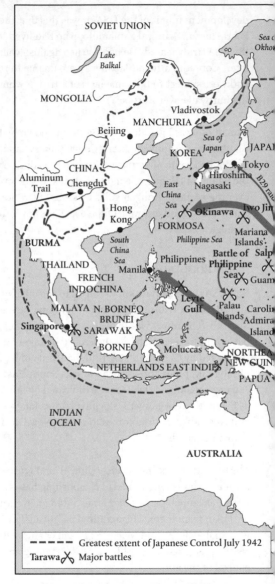

Aerial Warfare

6. WW2 in the Pacific took place over vast distances.

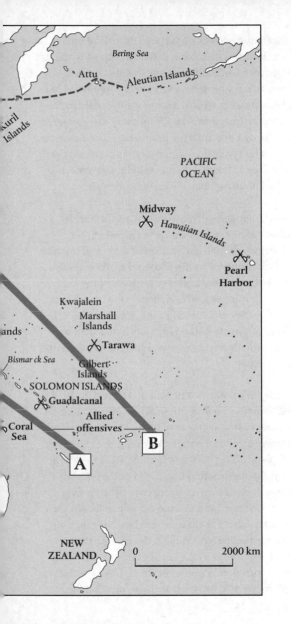

Guadalcanal, taken in November 1942, was the first of many hard-fought assaults on islands often defended almost to the last man by Japanese forces. Initially progress was slow, with a still-strong Japanese navy providing formidable opposition in a series of complex campaigns. Hard lessons were learned in these early assaults. By this time, however, US industry was running at full tilt, fulfilling its vast potential for production. The Americans ended the war with no fewer than ninety-eight aircraft carriers, including twenty-four of the excellent Essex class large fleet carriers. Japan had none capable of launching aircraft.

In October 1944 the Japanese resorted to the use of suicide attacks, designated 'kamikaze' (meaning 'divine wind')—a reference to a hurricane which had destroyed a Mongol invasion of Japan in the 13th century. Needless to say, kamikaze pilots' training was somewhat limited and they were easy prey for efficient shipborne gunfire as well as fighters. Only 11 per cent of kamikaze (or *Tokko*—'Special Attack' as the Japanese also called them) hit any kind of target. With every month that went by, US naval, marine, and air forces were ever larger and ever better equipped and trained.

In the Battle of the Philippine Sea in June 1944, the US Third and Fifth Fleets deployed no fewer than fifteen aircraft carriers against nine Japanese, sinking three of them. More importantly nearly 300 Japanese aircraft were shot down for the loss of just twenty-nine US planes. This battle, better known as the 'Great Marianas Turkey Shoot' proved to be the end of the formerly excellent Japanese fleet air arm as an effective fighting service. By February 1945, US naval and marine forces had fought their way up the Marianas Island chain to within bomber range of the Japanese islands themselves. Saipan, Guam, and Tinian, all within 1,500 miles of Japan (the range of the new US B-29 bombers), were captured. In a matter of weeks US Navy 'Seabees' (Construction Battalions, 'CBs') built air bases on all of them.

In April 1945, the Americans captured Okinawa, the first of the Japanese home islands to be taken, and casualties on both sides were very high. Planners now worked on Operation Downfall, the invasion of Japan. By this time, the cataclysmic air assault on Japanese cities had begun.

Strategic bombing in the Far East

The USA was developing options for the long-range bombing of Japan from 1941 when orders were placed for the huge Boeing B-29 bomber. This aircraft was a generation beyond anything that had gone before. With a pressurized crew compartment and remotely controlled gun turrets it was faster than most fighters, and had a fully loaded combat radius of 1,500 miles. It was the most expensive single conventional arms procurement project of WW2.

By early 1945 the US Navy's submarines and USAAF minelaying aircraft had effectively sealed Japan off from its overseas forces and supplies (Operation Starvation). Aircraft from carrier groups off the Japanese coasts destroyed military bases and industrial targets almost at will. If naval aircraft could attack the Japanese islands in numbers, what then was the role of the B-29? As matters were to demonstrate, it was here that ideas of undermining the will to fight of the civilian population were to reach something of an apotheosis.

The first combat raids on Japan took advantage of the Anglo-Indian success in retaking Burma in 1944. A huge logistics effort took fuel and equipment over the Himalayas (known as the 'Hump') from bases in India and Burma to Chengdu in China where a force of B-29s known as XX Bomber Command was based. It was here in the China–Burma–India theatre of operations that many of the techniques of mass air mobility were developed. This route was known as the 'aluminum trail' because of the number of crashes that occurred in the days before Brigadier

General William Tunner brought rather more efficiency to the effort. Search and rescue teams were deployed to recover downed airmen in these remote areas. The tactics and techniques they pioneered directly influence air search and rescue today. The supply effort over the 'Hump' became the greatest feat of air mobility before the Berlin Airlift in 1948, in which General Tunner also played a major role.

The XX Bomber Command raids on Japan from China in late 1944 and early 1945 were operating at extreme range, and did little lasting damage. Bases somewhat nearer to Japan, and rather more easily supplied, were by now being built. XXI Bomber Command was forming on freshly constructed bases on the recently captured northern Marianas Islands of Tinian and Saipan. XXI Bomber Command was initially commanded by a graduate of the ACTS, General Haywood Hansell, who had helped refine US bombing theory in the 1930s. Raids began on Japan in February but were disappointing. High-altitude precision bombing did not work over Japan; cloud cover and a persistent jet stream ensured that only a small proportion of bombs fell near their targets. Hansell was dismissed by the Chief of Staff of the US Army Air Force, General 'Hap' Arnold, and replaced by Curtis LeMay. LeMay developed a different tactic; instead of high-altitude bombing, all too often through cloud, he ordered his crews to fly at 5,000–9,000 feet, thus ensuring they could see their targets. Instead of using high explosive bombs, studies in the US had shown that Japanese cities were made mostly of wood, and would burn well. Therefore LeMay ordered that his aircraft have incendiary bombs as their main loads.

LeMay's hypothesis was proved very quickly on the night of 10–11 March 1945 when Operation Meetinghouse took 325 B-29s over Tokyo, destroying sixteen square miles of the city and killing 100,000 people. This was the deadliest raid in history, apart from the atomic bomb attacks. Over the next five months, sixty-seven

Japanese cities received similar treatment. By August 1945 over 300,000 people had been killed, probably far more—most were civilians. In mid-1945, Allied forces (predominantly American but with a significant British component) were preparing for an invasion of Japan.

The atomic raids

More was to come with the atomic raids, delivered by two B-29s of the 509th Bomb Group of the Twentieth Air Force. *Enola Gay*, piloted by Colonel Paul Tibbets, dropped 'Little Boy' on Hiroshima on 6 August 1945 (Figure 7). His co-pilot on that mission, Major Charles ('Chuck') Sweeney, flew *Bockscar* to Nagasaki on 8 August and dropped 'Fat Man'. Casualty figures for both atomic raids are unclear, but each killed at least 50,000 people instantly, probably very many more, and permanently disabled tens of thousands more. Japan surrendered shortly afterwards, as in the words of Emperor Hirohito in his statement to the nation, the war situation had 'not developed necessarily to Japan's advantage'. Three or four more atomic bombs would have been available by the end of September 1945; the intention was to continue dropping them until the Japanese capitulated.

The closely connected questions about the true motivation for the atomic attacks, and the degree to which they did in fact cause Japanese surrender, form one of the greatest controversies in the history of war. Some argue that the true purpose behind them was not to coerce Japan to surrender, but to demonstrate to the Soviet Union, now flexing its military might in China as well as Europe, that the USA had an atomic capability and could and would use it. They argue that the surrender of Japan was incidental, and that US leaders knew full well that Japan was on its knees and about to concede defeat. Others point out that the evidence for this is largely circumstantial; it is clear, they say, that Japanese leaders had declared that they would defend their homeland against invasion and that there would be no capitulation.

7. The world's first nuclear attack.

Here is not the place to rehearse in any detail the morality of the
conventional and atomic destruction of Japan's cities. It is worth
pointing out that unlike in Germany no argument was available
concerning diversion of resources to air defence or the war-winning
effects of the destruction of Japan's industry. The former was
irrelevant, since Japan did not have and failed to develop an
effective IADS which drew resources from other fronts. The latter,
destruction of useful industry and military infrastructure, had

partly been accomplished with the use of more precision but less fanfare by naval fighter-bombers operating from carrier groups. Similarly, as already stated, to all intents and purposes Japan had been sealed off as a potential resource for its overseas forces, so the annihilation of its infrastructure was primarily going to hit civilians. The Allies, particularly the Americans, were in the late stages of preparing Operation Downfall, the codename for the invasion of Japan. Had the Japanese not surrendered, Downfall would have begun in November 1945. Estimates of potential casualties ranged from about 500,000 to 1 million US and Allied service personnel. Estimates of possible Japanese casualties were far, far higher.

The US stance was summarized in a weekly intelligence brief of July 1945 for the Fifth Air Force fighting in the Western Pacific. It stated: 'The entire population of Japan is a proper military target. There are no civilians in Japan. We are making war and making it in the all-out fashion which saves American lives, shortens the agony which war is and seeks to bring about an enduring peace.' LeMay himself, who commanded the raids on Japan, put the case in his distinctive laconic fashion: 'No point in slaughtering civilians for the mere sake of slaughter...The entire population got into the act and worked to make those airplanes or munitions of war...men, women, children. We knew we were going to kill a lot of women and kids when we burned [a] town.' Readers will arrive at their own conclusions, first as to whether the campaign did succeed in its objective, and second as to its morality. The arguments continue in the literature and in the press.

Air power in WW2: a conclusion

Strategic bombing to coerce capitulation had failed in the combined operations against Germany. It seems likely now that the atomic raids contributed to rather than caused Japanese surrender.

Command of the air was indispensable, as Douhet had argued it would be. However, air power alone could not deliver success. When used as a component of an integrated pragmatically founded strategy, it was nonetheless vital. Although ideas that 'the bomber will always get through' proved unfounded, along with ideas of unescorted precision bombing, Mitchell and his followers were proved right to the extent that the selection of the right targets, rather than the obliteration of cities, might be highly effective. The decision at Casablanca in January 1943 to focus on gaining control of the skies by destroying the Luftwaffe in the air and denying it fuel and supplies on the ground and to resource the Battle of the Atlantic was the key to a successful invasion in the West.

Control of the air allowed the baleful arithmetic of attrition to act against a partially organized German industrial and military system under the stress of intense attack. Whilst well-planned and indeed commercially viable Western industrial strategies ensured overwhelming material superiority, excellent training guaranteed qualitative superiority in the air and on the ground. The practical and indeed political imperative to defend the Reich drew fighters from the Eastern Front and opened the way for the Soviets to gain and exploit control of the air and ultimately break the German army.

After 1940 Britain's industries were, if not immune to attack, then well defended. By 1943 success in the Atlantic, itself secured by excellent naval–air cooperation, guaranteed the supply of US materiel and reinforcements by sea. In the Pacific, US strategy—led by an extremely strong naval air component—defeated Japan in detail, not only by exploiting the fact of American industrial might but by developing a formidable operational and tactical skillset. That Japan had neither anticipated a long war nor set up an adequate support and training network only helped the US effort, as did the lack of any effective IADS, or any attempt to develop one. In August 1945, the last month of the war, US factories turned out 11,000 aircraft, the same number that Japan had lost in the previous two years.

Allied forces in almost every theatre leveraged their growing material preponderance by learning and adapting quickly. This was particularly clear in the field of support to ground forces. Good leadership fostered strong mutual recognition of the importance of both land and air components, the overriding importance of control of the air, and an understanding of each other's limitations. This in turn produced a realistic joint doctrine, the essence of which remains in place today.

Chapter 6
Cold War 1945–1982

In August 1945 a new conflict began between a new set of adversaries in the form of the largely liberal and capitalist West, led by the USA, and the Communist bloc led by the USSR. In his Fulton, Missouri speech of 5 March 1946, Winston Churchill, spoke of an 'Iron Curtain' descending across Europe, dividing the Communist states from those under the protection of the USA (most significantly, future members of NATO). It remained in place until 1989.

During the Cold War the USA and the USSR built vast fleets of aircraft. Export versions of US and Soviet planes equipped their respective allies, ensuring a high degree of standardization and a sure market for the latest designs. Aside from the USSR and the USA, only the United Kingdom and France maintained significant indigenous, high-end military aircraft programmes.

Attack

The USA built its air power around the United States Air Force (USAF) which, autonomous in all but name, received its long-awaited independence from the army in 1947. For much of the 1950s and 1960s, the USAF was dominated by Strategic Air

Command, which was set up to deliver the US nuclear deterrent. Under the command of Curtis LeMay, its aircraft patrolled the boundaries of Soviet airspace twenty-four hours a day, awaiting the call to go in and strike. By now, bombers on both sides, such as the vast Boeing B-52 or the Soviet Tupolev 95 Bear, had ranges of thousands of miles. Both remain in service today, and will so remain for decades to come. The USSR's equivalent to Strategic Air Command was its Long-Range Air Force although its aircraft were rarely on permanent patrol largely due to logistical limitations. Away from increasingly missile-dominated nuclear weaponry and the game-theorizing which developed around it, preparation for conventional war by the superpowers never stopped.

NATO and their Warsaw Pact adversaries, dominated by the USSR, faced each other in a state of heavily armed readiness across the plains of Central Europe. Both sides placed interdiction by aircraft at the heart of their operational plans. This required strike/attack aircraft to be able to fight their way at low level through formidable ground-based and air defences to cut their enemies from reinforcement and supply. This gave rise to specialist bombers such as the UK/German/Italian Panavia Tornado. Close air support, especially in the anti-tank role, was also felt to be a key role of air forces. The closer such support was to the front the better; the UK developed an aircraft that could fly from just behind the front lines, taking off and landing like a helicopter but flying low and fast, the Harrier. Despite the preponderance of hugely expensive equipment it was acknowledged more or less openly that if the Soviet forces attacked, sooner or later nuclear weapons would be used to stop them; these would be, in the parlance of the time, 'tactical' nuclear weapons. It was not until the 1980s that some serious thinking was applied to trying to win a conflict conventionally rather than assuming that the day would be saved, as it were, by obliterating the battlefield altogether.

Control of the air

Both main protagonists of the period and their allies and clients built and sustained huge fleets of jet fighters. These aircraft were armed with missiles (both radar-guided and heat-seeking) of ever-greater range and accuracy. The evolution of fighter technology was driven by the ferocious impetus of superpower competition, assisted of course from time to time by espionage and technical plagiarism. For example, a number of advanced British Rolls Royce Nene jet engines were sold to the Soviet Union in 1947 with the reservation that 'they not be used for military purposes'. The design was pilfered to power the outstanding MiG-15 jet fighters, to the great cost and consternation of many US aircrew during the Korean War. Concerning stolen designs, the first post-WW2 truly 'strategic' Soviet bomber, the Tupolev Tu-4, was a straight copy of the US Boeing B-29 Superfortress, some of which had been 'interned' when they had been forced to land in the USSR after being damaged in raids over Japan in 1945.

From the 1940s to the 1980s fighters were in constant development. Ever-faster single-role jets such as the US F-86 Sabre, the British Hawker Hunter, or indeed the Soviet MiG-15, all so-called 'first-generation' jet fighters, gave way to a second generation of supersonic interceptors designed to destroy high-flying bombers. These included the US F-104 Starfighter, the Soviet MiG-21, and the French Mirage III. In turn, combat experience, especially in the Middle East and Vietnam, proved the utility of 'multi-role' aircraft able to conduct strike missions and defend themselves like the fighter-bombers of WW2. Modified versions of these 'third generation' jets such as the McDonnell-Douglas F-15 or the Lockheed F-16 are still in widespread front-line combat service today. Indeed, the F-15 may claim to be the most successful of all fighters; pilots flying these fine aircraft for the US and Israeli air forces have achieved 100 kills and sustained no losses. During the Cold War great reliance was also placed upon GBAD, such as radar-guided anti-aircraft missiles. Belts of such missiles defended both NATO and Warsaw Pact territories.

Reconnaissance

All major air forces engaged in extensive strategic reconnaissance during the Cold War, especially the USA with its U-2 high-altitude spy planes. Two U-2s were shot down, one piloted by Gary Powers over the Soviet Union in 1961 (Powers was captured and later exchanged), and the other over Cuba on 27 October 1962 during the intense 'Missile Crisis'. It was vital for reconnaissance aircraft to be immune to fighters and missiles; it was for this reason that the US SR-71 Blackbird was brought into service, still, as far as we know from open sources, the fastest jet ever made. The SR-71 was given the ironic codename of 'Oxcart' as it was being developed. With its radar-deflective structure and materials the SR-71 was the first aircraft specifically designed to be stealthy.

As space exploration became more accessible in the 1960s, satellites took on this reconnaissance role. Even today, spy planes are still important elements for most air forces. Unlike satellites, whose orbits are often well known, the appearance of reconnaissance aircraft is unpredictable.

Strategic air mobility comes of age

Nowhere was Churchill's Iron Curtain more evident than in Berlin. It was here that the first major encounter of the Cold War took place. It was decided virtually without a shot fired and almost entirely by the application of air power. The Yalta Agreement of 1945 had placed the city, itself divided into four sectors, Soviet, US, UK, and French, deep within the Soviet zone of occupation. In June 1948, following the announcement of a new German currency, the Deutschmark, the land routes or 'corridors' from the West were sealed by order of Josef Stalin in an attempt to force Allied withdrawal and ensure Soviet control.

On the first day of the blockade the US Military Governor of Germany, Lucius Clay, ordered his Air Commander, Major General Curtis LeMay, to initiate an airlift from western Germany into Berlin. Once this had begun, President Truman gave the order, 'we're staying'. So began the Berlin airlift. From late 1943 to the end of the war Berlin had been subjected to a sustained and ferociously destructive bombardment by thousands of US, British, and other aircraft from the Western Allies. In 1948, many of those same bomber crews once again flew thousands of missions to the 'big city'; this time they were bringing not bombs, but food, fuel, and clothing; everything to sustain a huge city under siege. The airlift was managed by General William H. Tunner, who had successfully reorganized and run the airlift from India to China over the 'Hump' during 1944–5. The air routes remained open. Allied aircraft flew more than 5,000 tons of supplies into Berlin each day, including coal to heat the city during the winter. By May 1949 when the land routes opened, more than 2.3 million tons of supplies had been airlifted. West Berlin remained within the democratic fold. Air mobility deployed in great force had gained a strategic victory, the first of the Cold War.

The airlift provided the impetus for the development of purpose-built military transports, such as the C-130 Hercules. It also heralded the introduction of measures such as air traffic control corridors, used by every aircraft, civilian and military, today. Of more strategic importance, the Berlin airlift once again demonstrated not only that air power without firing a shot could have significant political impact. Throughout the Cold War, the power and potential of strategic airlift was demonstrated again and again, in Korea, the Middle East, and Vietnam.

New technology

In essence military aircraft served exactly the same role as their predecessors in WW2, only technology had changed. There were some true innovations in air power. Two come immediately to mind; effective air-to-air refuelling and the helicopter. Like control of the air or indeed reconnaissance, the former became one of the most important *enablers* in all first-class air forces' inventories. It allowed aircraft to reach targets or destinations that would be impossible using only internally stored fuel. Experiments in fuelling one aircraft from another had taken place as early as WW1, but it was not considered practicable until airframes powerful enough to carry sufficient fuel for several other aircraft were developed.

The second innovation offered a new form of aviation opportunity, particularly for ground commanders—vertical lift without the need for spacious airfields that were difficult to defend. Primitive models had been designed and indeed flown towards the end of WW2, but it was the tragic conflicts in South-East Asia and North Africa that proved their potential. By the late 1960s large helicopters could transport artillery; major powers now had hundreds of smaller transport helicopters in their inventories for carrying troops, medical evacuation, or indeed ground attack in support of land forces. At sea the helicopter had come of age; all major warships carried at least one, and sometimes two or more, armed with torpedoes or other anti-submarine or anti-ship missiles.

The absolute imperative for Cold War rivals and their respective allies to match and exceed each other's military capabilities ensured a high level of funding and investment in defence and particularly aerospace industries. On both sides of the Iron Curtain, the constant competition produced significant advances, the results of which brought air power into a new era.

The decades prior to the fall of the Berlin Wall saw great advances in electronic countermeasures (ECM). As we will see, the Middle Eastern wars demonstrated that there was a very great need for effective ECM against lethally efficient surface-to-air missile systems and indeed increasingly effective air-to-air missiles.

In the Vietnam War, ECM was used extensively against North Vietnamese air defences; for example USAF 'Wild Weasel' aircraft ranged the skies attempting to jam air defence radars—with considerable success.

During the 1970s and 1980s, the concept of IADS—so effective in WW2—was extended. Airborne early warning (AEW) aircraft were another innovation of the Cold War. Radar has a far greater range when mounted in aircraft flying at height. AEW aircraft such as the E3D AWACS (airborne warning and control system), developed from the Boeing 707 airliner, now form the heart of most major IADS systems. Fighter controllers are usually carried in these large aircraft, allowing for highly efficient direction of fighter resources. As crucial assets and high-value targets, AEW aircraft also need protection themselves.

Now the major powers were operating 'layered air defence systems'. In layered systems, radars detect incoming aircraft and jammers disrupt their guidance systems whilst SAMs engage them directly and fighters are also directed onto them. Nearer the objectives targeted by enemy aircraft, shorter range SAMs attempt to destroy surviving intruders. The objectives themselves are passively defended by ECM, and some are mobile or protected by physically hardened structures. Needless to say, the whole system is tied together by C3 with extensive redundancies and robust data links.

The Korean War

After 1945, major conflict between states remained relatively rare outside the Middle East and South Asia. An early exception was Korea (1950–3), where Communist North Korea had attacked South Korea, allied to the USA which led a coalition in response under the UN flag.

The Korean War was fought by a mix of mostly fighter aircraft, some powered by the new turbojet technology and some WW2-era propeller-driven aircraft. Air power was vital in ensuring that US-led forces eventually succeeded in driving back North Korean armies which were actively assisted by vast numbers of Chinese forces. The USSR also played a key role, and it was here that for the first and virtually last time US aircrew fought Soviet pilots (albeit flying North Korean-marked fighters). The Soviets denied any involvement and their pilots were careful never to cross front lines and risk capture if they were shot down.

US interdiction raids to disrupt Communist supply lines and heavy bombing of what little infrastructure and industry there was devastated North Korea. The USA could not, or would not, strike at China or Russia. To do so would certainly have initiated a full-scale open war with Communist powers. Accordingly, Communist forces in Korea itself always had secure strategic depth which was immune to strike, and they exploited this depth to sustain a little-known but remarkably enduring airlift of supplies from the USSR (using supply bases as far away as Europe) and China.

Following WW2, CAS skills had been neglected. The exception was the US Marine Corps where there was (and is) very close integration between air and ground elements. Consequently, many of the lessons of WW2 concerning cooperation and integration had to be learned again by the new USAF. This pattern of 'skill-fade', followed by relearning, has been a perennial problem for many air forces since WW2.

Control of the air over the battlefields was gained and held by UN/US forces over the entire peninsula; this allowed the first effective deployment of helicopters across the operational theatre, especially in the MEDEVAC role. It also, by the way, allowed the deployment for the first time of combat search and rescue helicopter missions to recover downed aircrew deep in enemy territory. However, despite the US/UN success in gaining and retaining control of the air, occasional night-time nuisance raids were mounted by low-technology North Korean aircraft, many of them biplanes. On 15 April 1953, two US soldiers were killed in one of these raids; since then no US ground troops have died on any battlefield as a result of enemy air action.

Wars of national liberation 1945–1979

Resistance to occupation during WW2—for example, against German forces in the occupied USSR—had usually been dealt with by the application of great amounts of firepower and large numbers of ground forces. This pattern continued, although when Western (UK, US, and French) forces were opposing insurgencies it was occasionally cloaked with the rhetoric of 'hearts and minds'. Air power played a large role in all these wars, but was decisive in none.

After WW2, Britain, the largest of the European colonial powers, was tired and broke. Almost immediately the British found themselves fighting wars of colonial withdrawal, the most intense of which took place in Malaya. There the British and their allied colonial air forces defaulted to what they knew best—bombing. Many thousands of tons of high explosives were dropped, largely ineffectively, upon the forests of the Malay Peninsula.

Britain's many post-WW2 counterinsurgency wars were low-casualty and relatively low-intensity affairs. France's wars of imperial withdrawal were a very different matter. The French were determined to retain colonial governments in their main possessions in Vietnam and Algeria. The consequent wars were remarkable for the huge casualties inflicted, particularly upon the civilian populations. Air power made a significant contribution to those figures. Whilst the British had used helicopters in their counterinsurgency campaigns for small-scale troop insertions, it was the French who were the true pioneers of what is now termed 'airmobile forces', ground units moved by helicopter.

In the French Indo-China War (1946–54), available technology comprised little more than small machine-gun-armed helicopters in an attack role, along with occasional helicopter MEDEVAC (as the USA had in Korea). The French fought another major counterinsurgency in Algeria (1954–62). At the beginning of the war there was a single privately owned Bell helicopter in the country. As the Algerian war progressed flights of large US-supplied Vertol H-31 Flying Bananas (Figure 8) or Sikorski H-34 (known in British use as Whirlwinds) were able to drop an entire battalion of 600 paratroops or commandos on a position in less than half an hour. It was found quickly that these were vulnerable to anti-aircraft ground fire. So the helicopter gunship, armed with machine-guns and rockets, was born to cover these landings.

None of these efforts or those of the huge French ground forces deployed to Algeria brought success. The war ended with Algerian independence in 1961. Despite, or perhaps partly because of, the use of liberally applied force and its effect on civilian support, both from the air and on the ground, overwhelming military power

8. **Algeria 1956.**

had failed to defeat an opponent with a well-defined and popular political cause.

Wars raged in Africa throughout the Cold War period. Air power played a significant role in Angola (1961–75) and Mozambique (1964–74) as Portugal tried unsuccessfully to suppress insurgencies. The small Rhodesian Air Force used their aircraft very efficiently in the Zimbabwean War of Independence (1964–79, also known as the Rhodesian Bush War or the Second Chimurenga). It was very rare for insurgent forces to use aircraft; however, during the Biafran War (1967–70), mercenary pilots flying for the separatist Biafran Army caused major problems for their Nigerian opponents.

The Vietnam War

However deadly the 1950s wars of colonial withdrawal were, they seemed only a prelude for what 1960s Indo-China was to provide. The fate of the French in Vietnam had been decided by their defeat at the Battle of Dien Bien Phu (1954). Following the French surrender, the country was partitioned into Communist North and a corrupt democratic government in the South, allied with the USA.

The new US-backed state of South Vietnam faced an insurgency from the National Liberation Front (NLF, also known as the 'Viet Cong'). Strong support was supplied by North Vietnamese regular forces (North Vietnamese Army (NVA)) in turn supplied by both China and the USSR. The USA was keen to avoid the prospect of states falling serially under Communist control under what was called the 'domino theory'. During the 1960s, the USA gradually increased its military involvement in Vietnam. By 1968, more than 500,000 American troops were deployed to Vietnam. The supporting air campaign was by far the largest in the post-WW2 period.

Building on their own and French experience, the USA had developed the concept of the helicopter-borne air mobile division rather than the mere battalion (1,000 or so combatants) that the French had managed in Algeria. Now an entire division (several thousand troops) could be landed very quickly on a given position, assuming the landing zone was reasonably clear of enemy ground fire. Rarely were such a number dropped in this way. The famous battle of Ia Drang (14–15 November 1965, the subject of the film *We Were Soldiers*) was one example.

Ground movement was slow and often dangerous, so as the war in Vietnam progressed troops were very often moved into combat by air. One problem with this approach is that any military presence is often temporary; in one sense soldiers 'commute' to battle; this is a problem still today in counterinsurgency conflicts where there are insufficient troops to take *and hold* ground.

Another problem was, and is, that helicopters are vulnerable as they come in to land. In Vietnam NLF insurgents, armed at best with heavy machine guns, shot down over 3,300 Bell HU-1B Huey helicopters, the workhorse of the US army (who operated most of the helicopters in Vietnam) representing 45 per cent of the 7,013 deployed. Nearly 1,800 other helicopters were also shot down, proving again that control of the air could effectively be challenged from the ground.

One of the many remarkable features of the war was the extensive use of aircraft designed for high-end combat against poorly armed insurgents. These ranged from the huge B-52 bombers to an array of sleek, fast supersonic fighters. American soldiers, who directed them onto their targets, called the fighter-bombers 'fast-movers' and still do. As in Algeria, helicopters were used for CAS, especially Hueys, armed with rockets and machine guns. The US army had to wait until 1968 for the first rotary-wing aircraft specifically designed for ground-attack, the AH-1G Cobra.

'Rolling Thunder' and the 'Linebackers'

Whilst combat in South Vietnam was intense, the bulk of the bombing, codenamed Operation Rolling Thunder, was carried out on the supply routes from North Vietnam to the Viet Cong fighters of the South—the 'Ho Chi Minh trail'. The trail (actually thousands of individual small paths) often passed through Cambodia and Laos (Box 4). This complex system was known to the North Vietnamese as 'Route 559', named after 'Group 559', the

Box 4 The most heavily bombed country on earth

During the Vietnam War, US aircraft dropped about 7.6 million tons of bombs on South-East Asian countries. About 70,000 civilians were killed in North Vietnam alone.

The Allies dropped about 3.4 million tons of bombs on all targets in WW2, including 2.7 million tons on Germany. From 1964 to 1973, Laos, which was formally neutral, was hit by about 2.5 million tons of high explosives. Roughly one ton of bombs was dropped for every Laotian citizen, making it per capita by far the most heavily bombed country on earth.

During the course of 580,000 bombing sorties over Laos, 270 million sub-munitions (also known as cluster-bomblets) were delivered in Operations Barrel Roll and Steel Tiger. Thirty per cent of these did not explode. Since the war, more than 20,000 people have been killed by them. More than fifty people are still killed every year, very few of whom were born at the time of the war. Forty per cent of the victims are children. Laos has suffered more than half of all the world's cluster-bomb casualties.

The bombing cost $17 million *per day* in 2017 inflation-adjusted dollars, a greater amount than international aid agencies contribute annually to clear the mess.

unit responsible for managing the infiltration of weapons and stores to the South. The USA had only the haziest idea of the effect their bombing was having—they had no reliable data. The reality was that the trails could easily be moved or rebuilt, and the means of supply, human labour and trucks, were extremely resilient, easily replaced, and difficult to hit. Further, the South Vietnamese Communist Viet Cong insurgents lived largely off the land. It has been estimated that the Viet Cong required no more than thirty-four tons of supplies a day from the North to maintain its effort.

The bombing of the Ho Chi Minh trail and North Vietnam itself, whose key installations were specifically previously excluded from attack by order of the US president, intensified with Operations Linebacker I and Linebacker II in 1972–3. It is arguable that Linebacker II, a ten-day campaign in December 1972 (often termed 'the Christmas Bombings'), brought the North Vietnamese to the negotiating table. In that sense it was the only successful strategic bombing campaign of the Cold War period. Having said that, to some extent the North Vietnamese played into US hands by transitioning to conventional warfare using tanks and other mechanized equipment. This meant that their logistical chain was far more complex and therefore more easily and effectively attacked. At no point prior to 1972 were Communist forces vulnerable to that form of conventional attack.

US bombers were ferociously opposed by Soviet supplied SA-2 and SA-3 ground-to-air missile systems, radar guided AAA, and MiG fighters of the North Vietnamese air force. Despite the technical gap between the USA and North Vietnam, the USAF lost 1,737 fixed wing aircraft and the US Navy 530 during the war. The vast majority were shot down by ground fire of one kind or another.

Conceptually, Vietnam represented the nadir of air power thinking. The senior USAF commanders were students of the 1930s ACTS. As Mark Clodfelter wrote in his study of the US air campaign in Vietnam, *The Limits of Air Power* (1989), the USAF 'remained structured around ACTS tenets'. Further, Vietnam presented a fundamental challenge to the idea that air power could win wars.

The Arab–Israeli wars 1947–1982

Arguably the most successful air arm of the post-WW2 era was the Israeli Air Force (IAF). There were several reasons for this. First, Israel was surrounded by what amounted to enemy states and consequently defence was *the* national priority. Much of its population and effort was engaged in manning and supporting its defence forces. Operationally it consciously elected to adopt the offensive and in so doing ensured that, usually, it retained the initiative. For this reason the air force was and still is Israel's primary weapon.

Founded just before the 1947 War of Independence, the IAF was never a separate force like its RAF and USAF relatives. However, the IAF does have a distinctive ethos formulated in the 1950s by its first Chiefs of Staff Dan Tolkowsky (commander of the IAF 1953–8) and Ezer Weizman (commander 1958–66). Both had served in the RAF during WW2.

Tolkowsky was greatly influenced by his WW2 experience, both in the way that the RAF conducted its tactical operations in the Western Desert Campaign (working extremely closely with its land forces) and in its later adoption of the fighter-bomber. This suited a comparatively poor country which simply could not afford to have an extensive suite of aircraft with different roles. Further, both he and Weizman realized that there was no future for Israel in an attritional defence. Israel, being a narrow country, was and is very vulnerable to attack; it simply did not have the strategic depth for a costly defence involving manoeuvre and the exchange of territory for time. Consequently, Israel had to adopt a policy of forward defence that might take the form, when appropriate, of pre-emptive strikes. Accordingly, from the start great stress was placed upon recruiting very high-quality personnel; the IAF received, and continues to receive, the best and brightest of each year's conscription cadre.

From the beginning Israel has used its air force to great effect, cooperating closely with intelligence assets as well as ground forces. For example on 28 October 1956 in an action redolent of Operation Vengeance, the American killing of Admiral Yamamoto in 1943 (see Chapter 5), the nascent IAF shot down an Ilyushin Il 14 aircraft carrying most of the Egyptian army general staff. They had identified its timing and route through signals intelligence. The next day Israeli forces, supported by British and French troops, began the Suez War and routed the Egyptian army. Throughout the 1960s Egyptian and Israeli forces regularly clashed. Israel's air force was heavily outnumbered by its adversaries in Egypt, Syria, and Jordan. One solution to this was to focus, as the Israelis did and as an outnumbered RAF had done during the Battle of Britain, on the 'sortie-rate'—the number of missions flown, of their aircraft. This required a fast turnaround of aircraft—refuelling and rearming—another example of force-multiplication.

A plan was devised to ensure air control before ground combat was joined. Operation Moked ('Focus') was designed to neutralize the enemy's air force before it could take off, although the intention was to knock out the runways rather than destroy aircraft. In June 1967, Israeli intelligence determined that Egyptian and Syrian forces were planning a full-scale attack on Israel. Moked swung into action at 08.45 on 6 June 1967. In addition to making runways unusable, the first hour of the Israeli attack destroyed 200 Egyptian air force aircraft, most of them modern Russian jets, eliminating the threat they posed. During the ensuing Six Day War, Israeli aircraft annihilated Egyptian and Syrian ground forces. It was, as USAF officer and theorist John Warden said, 'the only war of the 20th century decided by a single battle on a single day'. To the enthusiast of air doctrine history, this surely was Douhet in action—control of the air was gained by destroying the enemy's bases. By the end of the war Israeli aircraft had destroyed nearly 80 per cent of Egyptian, Syrian, and Jordanian fighters and bombers. 'Moked' remains the best example of an effective OCA campaign.

Following this debacle, the Egyptians focused the reconstruction of their devastated air defences upon surface to air missiles. They deployed dozens of batteries of Soviet SA-2 (with a maximum range of 45 km) SA-3 and SA-6 SAMs with ranges of 25 km and 35 km respectively) (Figure 9). Soviet crews were often imported with them. This emphasis on the use of SAMs was partly dictated by the difficulties in resourcing and training capable aircrew, and partly because SAMs were cheaper than jets; but the primary attraction was that they were assessed to be more effective and efficient. The War of Attrition, desultory combat from 1967 to 1970 during which time Egypt received extensive and active support from the USSR, established SAMs as a significant new factor in the region. When full-scale war broke out again in October 1973, the audacious Egyptian crossing of the Suez Canal, surprising Israeli forces, was effectively covered by Egyptian SAM belts which inflicted heavy losses on Israeli jets. The confusion caused by these attacks was such that Israeli plans to deal with the

9. Soviet-supplied SA-3 anti-aircraft missile.

SAM sites (codenamed Operations Dugman and Tegar) were not successfully carried out. Control of the air over the Suez battlefield was effectively lost and only regained several days later when ground forces assaulted the SAM batteries and cleared gaps through which Israeli jets were able to engage Egyptian forces.

A simultaneous assault by Syrian forces on the disputed Golan Heights on the northern borders of Israel came perilously close to breaking though Israeli lines. Israeli doctrine closely followed well-established traditions of centralized control, so air assets were quickly switched from Suez to the Golan front, where they suffered heavy casualties from ground fire. The line just held, largely because the IAF interdicted Syrian fuel and ammunition dumps. The penalty of centralized control was that individual attacks had to be cleared by higher command, although in typical Israeli fashion local initiative and flexibility solved some of those problems. Meanwhile, the USA was not about to allow its ally to fail. It conducted an airlift of F-4 jets, amongst other materiel, to replace Israeli air losses; these aircraft were soon in the air. Prime Minister Golda Meir was blunt in declaring that this airlift had 'saved Israel'. Similarly, the USSR demonstrated its resolve to preserve the Egyptian state with an airlift of more Russian 'technicians' and indeed ground troops. A ceasefire was called to avoid escalation. In 1979, Egypt and Israel signed a peace deal which has held to this day.

The Israelis realized that they now faced a serious challenge from ground-based missile systems that had come very close to being strategically as well as tactically lethal. As Ezer Weizman, IAF commander, said, 'the missile has bent the aircraft's wing in this war; this fact should be analysed closely'. The IAF spent the next decade doing exactly that with excellent results. In Operation Arzav (Mole Cricket) in June 1982, Israeli drones electronically fitted to imitate fast-jet attack profiles were attacked by Syrian SAM batteries over the Beka'a Valley in Lebanon. Syrian SAMs were launched revealing the locations of their launchers' radars which were duly destroyed by Israeli missiles. Over the next week, Syrian MiGs, including top of the range MiG-21s, were dispatched to counter a concerted Israeli attack on the SAM systems. Israeli electronic warfare troops jammed Syrian communications and avionics rendering the planes easy prey for Israeli fighters. It was one of the most one-sided air battles in history, with up to eighty Syrian MiGs shot down. The Israelis lost just four jets to SAMs. Although drones had been used in Vietnam (in Project Snoopy to spot for naval guns), for the first time drones took a major role in air warfare. Like the Battle of Britain, the 1982 war over Lebanon was as much a victory for the Israeli *system* comprising new doctrines, technology, and organization, as it was a success of Israeli aircraft and pilots.

The Indo-Pakistan wars 1947–1971

Far away in South Asia another enduring post-WW2 rivalry was playing out. After WW2 the messy partition of British India had left, to put it mildly, a bitter legacy, with India divided into two now hostile states, India and Pakistan. Wars were fought in 1947–8, 1965, 1971, and 1999. As with the case of Israel, the experience of WW2 had been highly influential. Officers of both the Pakistan and Indian air forces had served in several theatres of that war, particularly Burma, where aircraft were vital in ensuring the transport and resupply of troops into difficult areas. Mehar Singh and K. L. Bhatia, who had both served as RAF pilots during WW2, would lead the Indian air force's transport fleet in the years after independence. The lessons they had learned were vital in securing Kashmir for India in November 1948 when four battalions of Indian infantry were airlifted into Srinagar, enabling Indian forces to hold the provincial capital.

In the next conflict of 1965 problems of command and coordination as well as a lack of political will to engage the full force particularly of India's quite considerable air arsenal prevented a decisive air intervention from either side. This was not the case in 1971, when Indian forces intervened convincingly in what was then called East Pakistan.

Throughout 1971, East Pakistan (which was to become Bangladesh) had suffered severely from the depredations of forces from what is now Pakistan following moves towards independence. Tens of thousands of people had been killed, injured, and raped in a programme of ethnic cleansing. In November 1971, Indian Prime Minister Indira Gandhi ordered her forces under General Manekshaw to intervene openly in East Pakistan and then in Pakistan proper. Over a period of less than a month, they won a decisive victory wherein air power played a major role.

India had learned major lessons from previous conflicts, not least the necessity to ensure adequate CAS by deploying forward air controllers with army units. Helicopters were used extensively, as in Vietnam. As if to emphasize the ability of Indian forces to operate jointly, its aircraft carrier the INS *Vikrant* (formerly the British HMS *Hercules*), which had been enforcing a sea blockade, launched dozens of sorties in support of the Indian land campaign. The decisive air operation was a precision strike by Indian air force MiG-21s on Government House in Dhaka. This act of intimidation was 'the last psychological blow to a crumbling regime'. East Pakistan became Bangladesh the following year.

Air power and the maritime domain

The end of WW2 had cemented the role of aircraft carriers as the capital ships of any major navy. The USA constructed a fleet of huge nuclear-powered ships, each capable of carrying over 100 jet aircraft, many of them capable of nuclear attack. These formidable assets formed the heart of 'carrier groups' which could be sent to project US power or support US or indeed allied forces already in action. In both Korea and Vietnam carrier-borne aircraft played a significant role, although in both conflicts there were problems of command and coordination with air force counterparts, as naval command systems and cultures differed markedly from air force structures.

The United States Navy expanded the reach of its naval aviation to the point where it was—and remains—'the point of the spear' for US involvement in various conflicts. Other powers have maintained some carrier capability, notably France, India, and the United Kingdom. In the 1950s the Royal Navy pioneered the angled landing decks, steam catapults, and mirror landing systems still seen on large aircraft carriers today. These inventions allow jet aircraft to be launched and landed far more safely and efficiently, both of which are a vital capability in an environment where 'sortie-generation', the ability to get aircraft away quickly, is a crucial force-multiplier.

The UK, however, made the decision in the late 1960s to abandon its ambitions to be a major naval air power, and rely instead on land-based air power for its global strategic reach. In 1982, the Royal Navy's air power comprised only two small aircraft carriers, both equipped only to launch relatively short-range Sea Harrier jump jets. Early that year, Argentina resorted to force to solve the long-running dispute it had with Britain over the remote Falkland Islands (called by Argentina the Malvinas Islands) in the south Atlantic, about 400 miles from the Argentine coast. They invaded and occupied the islands in April 1982 and the UK quickly mounted a task force around its aircraft carriers. It was fully understood that command of the air would be a decisive factor for success. Unfortunately for Argentina, its air force, the Fuerza Aerea Argentina (FAA), was only informed of the operation two weeks before it was executed and had little time either to consider how to fight the conflict or indeed take part in its planning. Further, it had been forbidden to train over the sea as this was considered the navy's role. The Argentinian navy was taken out of the fight early in the war when a British submarine sank an Argentine cruiser, the *General Belgrano*, after which the country's only aircraft carrier returned to safe waters.

In May 1982, having established an exclusion zone (essentially a siege) around the islands, the British task force fought battles with the FAA to secure control of the air and ensure that the landings of ground troops could be accomplished without great loss. Shipborne defences shot down several FAA aircraft, but the burden of securing control of the air fell on the Royal Navy Sea Harriers. They were assisted by the fact that the FAA had not established an effective base on the Falklands; consequently Argentine fighters and strike aircraft were flying at the limit of their range, whereas Royal Navy air bases (the carriers) were far closer to the islands. Further, the Argentinians had no clear 'air picture' from the limited mobile radar that had been deployed to the Falklands. The British were somewhat constrained too by a lack of long-range radar, their AEW aircraft having gone the way of the Royal Navy's large aircraft carriers, the last of which was decommissioned in 1979.

The FAA, and indeed land-based Argentine navy aircraft (the latter armed with anti-ship missiles), prosecuted their attacks with courage and determination and were resisted in like fashion. They took a dire toll on British ships, sinking no fewer than five. In due course British troops landed and defeated the occupying Argentine forces. The Falklands War proved the need for effective airborne defence systems—in the form of fighters—for any ships deployed within range of aircraft, which is to say almost anywhere. It was also significant in that there were virtually no civilian casualties. This was a war fought between two military forces in an environment where there were very few civilians. Air power had been an essential component in the successful retaking of the islands.

Conclusion

The years of the 'deep' Cold War demonstrated time and again that the same lessons needed to be learned and relearned. First amongst these from a conventional air power perspective was the requirement for CAS and the procedures ensuring that it worked. Western aircraft largely proved themselves superior in capability to Soviet designs, but were very vulnerable to anti-aircraft artillery and SAMs which shot down 97 per cent of US aircraft (including helicopters) lost in Vietnam and 90 per cent of Israeli aircraft lost in the Arab–Israeli wars.

It can fairly be said that the period from 1945 to 1982 set the technical stage for the subsequent four decades; the replacement of piston-engines by jets vastly increased the reach, power, and indeed persistence of all types of aircraft. Precision weapons were becoming a vital part of the air inventory of serious wielders of air power. The potential of air mobility became readily apparent. At the strategic level in supplying cities under effective siege, or inserting critically needed reinforcements at the right time, or at the tactical level to move, supply, or evacuate large numbers of troops in combat, air mobility came to be seen rightly as one of the most important facets of air power.

Chapter 7
The apotheosis of air power 1983–2001

The period immediately after Vietnam saw little new thinking in the application of air power. As Mark Clodfelter has put it, technology had created 'a modern vision of air power that focusses on the lethality of its weaponry rather than that of the weaponry's effectiveness as a political instrument'. The means had been divorced from the ends.

This chapter examines how this changed. After examining briefly the new ideas encapsulated by the term 'manoeuvre warfare' we will look at some of the capabilities that made it happen, particularly precision and stealth. We will go on to look at several campaigns which saw air power used as the main military instrument. Many commentators see this period as the age when air power truly came into its own as an instrument of state power and indeed coercion.

During the 1980s there was something of a renaissance of doctrinal thinking led by two very different characters, John Boyd and John Warden. To adopt the terminology of the Norwegian scholar of air power John Olsen, Boyd taught practitioners how to think, Warden showed them how to act.

Boyd, a fighter pilot and maverick military theorist, saw parties to a war as 'complex adaptive systems'. The aim of an effective operator should be to inhibit the enemy's capacity to adapt to an ever evolving and shifting combat environment, resulting in confusion and over-reaction or indeed stunned passivity: 'He who can handle the quickest rate of change survives,' and this was likely to be effected by whoever could most efficiently go through the cycle of Observe, Orientate, Decide, and Act; this was framed as the 'OODA Loop' (Figure 10). It was the role of a military leader to prevent or inhibit the enemy from going through his own OODA loop, in other words to 'get inside' it. Now something of a commonplace of military colleges and business schools, the ideas embedded in the OODA loop represented a real shift in military thinking at the time.

Boyd himself never wrote a book on his ideas. However his influence has been very great on late 20th-century military thinking. He was part of a wider group within US and UK military circles championing the view that the threat to Western interests presented by the Soviet Union and the Warsaw Pact might effectively be countered by conventional means. Since the 1950s, NATO doctrine assumed that the Western alliance was so outnumbered by Warsaw Pact forces that it would eventually have to use nuclear weapons to deal with them. 'Not so,' said the new thinkers; Soviet forces *could* be defeated if NATO assets were used in the right way.

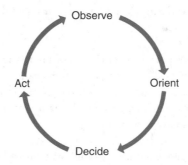

10. The OODA Loop.

Their new approach became known as 'manoeuvre warfare'. The central idea is that a numerically superior enemy can be defeated if his systems of communication are disrupted to the extent that the forces nearer to the front line begin to lose effectiveness and cohesion. Crucial to this is the idea of deep interdiction—stopping supplies and reinforcements reaching engaged units. In effect it might be characterized either as a defensive version of blitzkrieg, or a resurrection of some of the concepts of strategic interdiction developed in Western Europe in WW2. Boyd had described *what* intelligent application of military force might be able to do. Warden was to describe *how* air power might be used to do it.

Warden and neoclassical air power theory

USAF Colonel John Warden's best-known work is *The Air Campaign*, a short but clear exposition of air power as a strategic instrument. In its organization and to a lesser extent ambition, it is redolent of Clausewitz's *On War*. Warden himself saw it as a codex to the Russo-American theorist Alexander de Seversky's *Victory through Air Power* which was influential in US circles in the 1930s and 1940s. He uses examples from the last century of military history to illustrate how air power can be used at all levels.

Warden argues that the perspective of the air commander is and should be entirely different from that of the ground general. In a joint environment, the air commander will tend to be pulled back to the battlefield: 'If a rational campaign is to be carried out, an air force must have freedom to do it.' This approach has become known as 'neoclassical' air power theory, on the premise that Douhet and the ACTS represented 'classical' theory. There was one key difference: the ACTS approach centres around attempting to paralyse industrial production whereas Warden focuses on *political and command* paralysis. Warden retains, however, a stress on eliminating the enemy's air force and his bases—offensive counter-air.

Warden takes air power theory beyond Douhet in arguing that air power can be seen not as superior to but genuinely the equal of the other arms; each service should 'do what it is naturally constituted to do, and what only it is capable of doing'. Orchestration, not subordination or even integration, is the *sine qua non* of modern warfare. However, Warden argues strongly that air power can, in the right circumstances, be *the* key force. This is a controversial approach, not shared by many army and navy officers.

Warden reminds his readers that Douhet's insight was to try to circumvent by exploiting command of the air, Clausewitz's *Schlacht*—battle and combat. Douhet's was a direct approach, in other words to go directly for the strategic objective, which does not lie on the battlefield—the political decision-maker. This, in essence, meant the state and its leadership. Warden sees the modern state as a 'system of systems' and situated this within a framework of 'five rings' (Figure 11).

As the reader will see, sitting in the centre of this ring is the decision-maker—the strategic heart of a state. The outer four

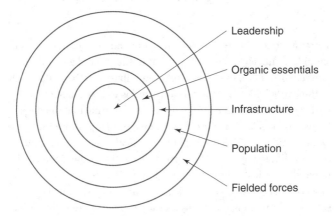

Leadership

Organic essentials

Infrastructure

Population

Fielded forces

11. Warden's Rings.

rings should be attacked only to facilitate dealing with that inner ring. In one sense this approach lies squarely within the tradition founded by the ACTS. One view might be that this is the interwar ACTS's industrial web theory applied to the entire strategic state.

The rise of precision

For manoeuvre warfare to work properly, for the necessary targets comprising Warden's Rings, for example, to be hit, precision was required to ensure that effort was not wasted. Fleets of bomber aircraft had attacked targets with 'dumb' (unguided) bombs in all conflicts. Where there are large formations of troops, tanks, or armoured vehicles this may still be an option, even today. Rather more pointedly, such missions are unnecessary and wasteful if the bombs miss their targets. Not least there are the political, legal, and moral problems caused by so-called 'collateral damage' to civilians.

The search for accurate means of delivery of high explosives has gone on since WW1. Precision makes economic and military sense. During WW2 and thereafter there were many precision raids whose effectiveness depended more upon intense training of crews than the technology of the ordnance being delivered. The next step in precision was to have weapons that could be guided once they had left the aircraft ontospecific targets such as bridges, ships, or individual buildings. TV and radar have been developed as means of guidance since the 1940s. A major advance took place with the thirty-one GPS satellites developed during the 1970s, launched into space in the 1980s, and fully operational by the 1990s. Originally intended as aids to navigation, they are now often used to guide missiles and bombs onto their targets.

By 1990, air commanders could assure their political masters that targets could be hit so accurately, where required, that they could guarantee very low civilian casualties (collateral damage). The question of collateral damage and the consequent imperative for using PGMs became more pressing as the years went on. The increase in precision was incremental. USAF General Michael Dugan observed that it took 4,500 WW2 B-17 Flying Fortress missions, ninety-five Vietnam War-era F-105 missions, and one single F-117 Stealth Fighter mission to ensure a single target's destruction.

These advances have allowed for targets identified by a dynamic and well-organized ISTAR system to be struck quickly thereby creating problems for the enemy's ability to adapt to the situation—to orient and decide. The tools for delivering the bombs themselves were to be fast, low-flying fighter-bombers able to defend themselves. John Boyd and his acolytes, known in some quarters as the 'fighter mafia' (the old 'bomber mafia' generals were now retired), were instrumental in ensuring that these aircraft were designed and built. These aircraft, the McDonnell Douglas F-15 Eagle and F-18 Hornet, and Lockheed F-16 Fighting Falcon, are still in front-line service all over the world.

Stealth, reconnaissance, and intelligence

Options for breaking down the enemy's key defence systems and getting through to a target might include destroying their command and control systems, shooting down fighters and missiles, or jamming their radars. Another option is to hide from detection altogether. Huge resources have been invested in what has become known as 'stealth' technology. Of course there is nothing new in the idea of camouflage. With the development of radar, efforts began to conceal aircraft in other ways. This can be achieved, first, by altering the shape of the airframe to divert electromagnetic signals from radar receivers; or, second, by creating materials that absorb the radiation so that it is not returned. Studies had begun in Germany during the 1940s on the extremely difficult mathematical problem of trying to design surface geometries which reflect electromagnetic waves such as radar. The most important work was carried out by the German physicist Arnold Sommerfeld, whose pupils included the pioneer of quantum physics Werner Heisenberg.

Early attempts at stealth with reconnaissance aircraft such as the U-2 were unsuccessful. However, during the 1970s, designers at Lockheed's legendary secret design facility in California, known as the 'Skunk Works', rediscovered the ideas of physicists such as Sommerfeld. In due course they produced the F-117 Nighthawk, the world's first stealth aircraft, which became operational in 1983 (Figure 12). With its oddly angular lines one leading historian of science, Arthur Miller, has described the aircraft as a 'flying cubist sculpture'. It was not until 1988 that the fact of its existence was made public. Although it was known as the Stealth Fighter, it was really a strike aircraft—a bomber in other words. It was followed by the long-range B-2 Spirit strategic bomber. At over $1 billion per airframe, only twenty-one of the other-worldly-looking B-2s have been made. All have seen extensive service.

12. The F-117 Stealth fighter.

Utilizing the control of the air, new reconnaissance platforms were developed to penetrate the fog of war' on the ground and provide as full a picture as possible of enemy forces. The most effective such platform is the joint surveillance target attack radar system (JSTARS), a converted Boeing 707 airliner flying outside enemy airspace using radar and other detection systems at a range of up to 150 miles from the targets it is observing. It can track up to 250 vehicles at one time. Whilst a prototype was first used in the First Gulf War, its first deployment in action was as part of the peacekeeping mission in Bosnia-Herzegovina during the mid- to late 1990s.

The first major test in combat for Western air forces came not in Central Europe against the Soviet Union and Warsaw Pact as had been feared and expected. It came in the Middle East.

The Gulf wars in the air 1980–1991

For most of the last three decades, the region around the Arabian Gulf has seen a vast amount of conflict, including several major conventional wars. The first of these, the Iran–Iraq War, was started by the Iraqi dictator Saddam Hussein in 1980. Iran and Iraq used their air forces extensively, both in a battlefield role and in attacks on each other's cities and infrastructure. Iran had been armed by the USA prior to its Islamic Revolution in 1979 when assistance was cut off. Many of its air and ground crews had been trained in the USA. In the early years of the war, it used its fleet very effectively. However, sanctions on Iran imposed after the revolution began to bite; spares became scarce and Iranian industry could not yet fill that gap.

Nonetheless, it took several years for the Iraqi air force, armed largely with Soviet equipment and seriously damaged by these early clashes, to recover and regain the initiative in the skies. The war devolved into a brutal attritional war on the ground as Iran counterattacked into Iraq. The Iranians developed innovative ways to keep their excellent US-made airframes in service, including on one occasion using F-14 fighters as airborne C2 platforms. By 1988 Iraq, now supported by the USA and partially armed by France, began to take the initiative in the air and drove back Iranian forces on the ground. By the end of the war, over 500,000 people had been killed and both nations' military capabilities and economies had been shattered.

The First Gulf War

Partly in an attempt to divert Iraqi popular disquiet from their appalling economic situation, Saddam Hussein ordered an invasion of neighbouring Kuwait in November 1990. The emirate was an ally of the USA and a coalition was put together to drive Iraq back to its borders. The whole force was commanded by Norman Schwartzkopf. Under him was General Charles 'Chuck' Horner who commanded the 'Joint Force Air Component', dominated by the USAF but with contributions from many Western states.

Iraq was not only facing a formidably trained force equipped with the very latest technology and weaponry. That vast force was to be applied using some innovative strategic thinking. Colonel John Warden designed a campaign initially called Instant Thunder and presented it to General Horner. His plan was for a campaign against the Iraqi state—the decision-maker at the centre of his scheme of 'five rings'—which was to be waged *entirely* by air. Horner initially disliked it. A modified version of the plan was developed by a team led by Lieutenant-Colonel David Deptula which formed the core of the larger Operation Desert Storm to retake Kuwait. The result was a devastating display of what air power could do. Essentially, two separate operations took place. The first, which had evolved out of Instant Thunder, was directed at the strategic levels of Iraqi infrastructure. The original intention, of course, was to circumvent the need for a destructive and deadly battlefield clash and take a 'direct' approach to the

Iraqi state. The second was an assault from the air upon the Iraqi army in the field.

The air campaign began in January 1991. It lasted thirty-nine days and was followed by a short but very sharp land invasion of Kuwait which routed Iraqi forces and liberated Kuwait. After the first few hours of US and coalition air assault on its air defences, Iraq had lost the capacity to put up any effective air resistance. This opened a route for coalition bombers to strike at Iraq itself and the leadership, command, and control systems which controlled not only the state but Iraq's army deployed in the field. PGMs were used for 60 per cent of these missions. The assault rendered Iraq's leadership ineffective as a strategic actor as it was able neither to convey orders nor receive information. New technologies greatly assisted this process. E-3A Sentry AWACS aircraft had established a RAP and ensured full coordination between coalition forces. Extensive use of ECM blinded and paralysed Iraqi defences. Whilst stealth missions comprised only 2 per cent of sorties, their accurate bombing destroyed 40 per cent of the strategic leadership targets.

In terms of the amount of high explosive dropped, the 'strategic' portion of Operation Desert Storm was as nothing to what was visited upon Iraqi forces in and around Kuwait in the thirty-nine days of the air campaign. Thousands of tanks and armoured vehicles were destroyed by bombs and guided missiles, and tens of thousands of Iraqi servicemen were killed. This ferocious assault included, for the first time since the Vietnam War, the use of huge B-52 bombers in an 'area bombing' role against large formations of Iraqi troops and vehicles. Psychological warfare units designed operations around the air attacks, warning Iraqi troops of what would befall them if they failed to surrender; thousands of Iraq troops accordingly did surrender. Overall, only 9 per cent of all munitions used in the war were precision-guided. However, it was later assessed that 75 per cent of the serious *damage* to key Iraqi assets was caused by PGMs.

The First Gulf War is sometimes regarded as the conflict in which the potential of air power was fully realized. It is often argued that the war was won by it. There is no doubt that when the ground phase of Operation Desert Storm began, the task of UK, US, and French ground forces was made far more straightforward by the very great attrition air power had inflicted. It played a major role in ensuring that coalition casualties were acceptably low (fewer than 200 killed, many of them by friendly fire). Indeed, it has been said that it was statistically safer to be a soldier in the vast US and allied army deployed to the combat theatre than to live in New York.

It was a triumphant tactical and operational success. It has been seen as the ultimate vindication of the ideas of both Boyd and the manoeuvre warriors (although manoeuvre warfare tends to be regarded as having land and air assets working *concurrently*). The First Gulf War also represented the culmination of a great deal of training and preparation over the previous decade. Interestingly, it was the first conflict in which avoiding collateral damage became an important and compulsory feature of the targeting and planning process.

However, before accepting the argument that the First Gulf War was an unalloyed triumph of air power, the point should also be made that although some Iraqi units retreated *before* the invasion by coalition armies, Kuwait was *occupied by US and allied ground forces*. This was not a victory of air power alone. Clausewitz's rule that war must be decided on the battlefield surely remained intact. Whether the First Gulf War was the apotheosis of air power as some have argued, or a necessary adjunct to a joint operation, is a matter for historians. Air Vice-Marshal Tony Mason has pointed out that every possible advantage that could be enjoyed was present, not least weather, the flat terrain with few opportunities for concealment or camouflage, and the ready availability of air basing and fuelling facilities. The Iraqi armed forces were a generation behind in terms of technology, a fact of which the experienced Iraqi commanders were more than aware.

Further, to some extent, Iraqi forces (a large army and air force operating with Soviet weaponry and to a lesser extent Soviet doctrine) were precisely the kind of enemy that coalition forces had been set up, trained, prepared, and equipped to fight over the previous three decades. What is certain is that whilst it was, perhaps, not sufficient, at the very least the air campaign was necessary to the military success, demonstrating the devastating potential of the combination of superior equipment, well-trained and prepared forces, and innovative planning and doctrine.

Coercion in humanitarian war: the Balkan Wars 1991–1999

Although the First Gulf War is often seen as the high-point of strategic application of air power, perhaps a stronger candidate for that title lies elsewhere. The 1990s saw several wars of nationalism take the lives of tens of thousands in south-east Europe as the former Federal Republic of Yugoslavia fell apart. Between 1992 and 1995 the most deadly of these conflicts raged in Bosnia. UN forces were present on the ground and in the air; despite some successes in bringing humanitarian aid they were ineffective in moderating the savage genocidal violence. Matters came to a head in July 1995 when over 8,000 men and boys were murdered by Serbian forces in and around Srebrenica in the largest single massacre in Europe since the end of WW2. This galvanized the USA and European members of NATO into action. Over a period of less than a month from late August to late September 1995, NATO forces delivered a series of air attacks, combined with artillery strikes codenamed Operation Deliberate Force. The effectiveness and ferocity of these sharp precision strikes upon deployed Serb forces (coupled with a Croatian ground assault) brought the Bosnian Serbs and their sponsor President Milošević of Serbia himself to the negotiating table. The resulting Dayton Accords of December 1995 ended the Bosnian War.

The Dayton Accords did not resolve the long-standing problem of Kosovo, a province in southern Serbia with a large majority of ethnic Albanians. Over the previous decade repression by Serbian authorities had caused a low-level insurgency between separatist Albanian insurgents, the Kosovo Liberation Army, and Serbian security forces. In 1998 full-scale conflict broke out. After the expulsion of a peacekeeping mission in March 1999, NATO began an air campaign, Operation Allied Force, to coerce Serbian authorities to accept defined terms. Meanwhile, a campaign of Serbian ethnic cleansing of Kosovan Albanians, already firmly in process, was intensified. It was assumed that a short, sharp campaign would be sufficient as it had been in Bosnia. NATO, however, underestimated the political will of Milošević, who regarded Kosovo as far more important to Serbia than Bosnia. Operation Allied Force lasted seventy-eight days before Milošević agreed to NATO's terms. President Clinton had explicitly rejected the option of a ground invasion early in the war so Operation Allied Force was conducted entirely from the air. No NATO casualties were sustained—a vital element for the retention of fragile public support in NATO countries, especially the USA.

The Kosovo air campaign was marked by a degree of confusion as to targeting priorities. Initially, the main targets were Serbian forces deployed in Kosovo, much as had been the case in Bosnia, and the campaign was expected to be short. It took weeks for allied planners to identify the key target set or 'centre of gravity'. Success came only with a strategic campaign against key Serbian infrastructure such as bridges and power stations and, eventually, industries in which Milošević and his clan held financial interests (e.g. cigarette factories). Very well-trained and prepared Serbian GBAD personnel had studied the NATO air campaigns over Iraq and Bosnia. Equipped at best with 1980s technology, they concluded that there was little future in trying to compete with NATO on its own terms, a view consolidated when five of their most advanced MiG-29 fighters were shot down in short order.

Serbian forces launched over 800 SAMs and succeeded in forcing NATO aircraft to fly very high (over 15,000 feet) to avoid them. NATO sustained no significant casualties although two aircraft were shot down, both by the 3rd Battalion of Serbia's 250th Missile Brigade commanded by one Colonel Zoltan Dani. Most significant was an F-117 Stealth Fighter shot down by 1960s vintage SA-3 missiles. Dani successfully directed the strengths of the low-frequency P18 radar (NATO codename 'Spoon Rest', a 1956 design) against the weaknesses (low speed and visual observability) of the F-117 Stealth platform. Colonel Dani is now retired and runs a bakery.

Air power advocates tout Kosovo, like the First Gulf War, as an example of how well-directed precision air strikes can achieve strategic effects. However, there is another side to the story. Milošević capitulated when Russia threatened to withdraw support and the ethnic cleansing campaign was not playing well in international media. Further, US President Clinton had removed the restriction he had imposed against a NATO ground invasion of Serbia. Accordingly the threat of direct regime change became rather more immediate. Whilst the threat of ground invasion had, perhaps, tipped Milošević over the edge, it was the air campaign that had taken him to that edge.

Strategic theorist Thomas Schelling has said that in using coercion, 'the threat of violence in reserve is more important than the commitment of forces in the field'. In Kosovo, NATO gradually increased the levels of force used, with the understanding that there was always more available.

Conclusion

The late 20th century might realistically be argued to be the apogee of air power used 'alone'. Of course any idea that air power can be used alone is a fallacy. No war has ever been fought entirely from the air. However, there is no doubt that in the First Gulf War, the potential of air power, intelligently and ruthlessly delivered, was demonstrated. In Bosnia and subsequently Kosovo, air power had been highly significant, to say the very least.

The history of the last century of air power has demonstrated that if military force is going to be deployed *without* air power, success—whatever that is judged to be—is unlikely. Certainly, if your opponent has an air force and you do not, or you lose the battle in the air, you are likely to lose the battle on the ground (or at sea) and very likely to go on to lose your war. The single exception to this rule, and it is a significant one, is the rather special case of insurgency. The USA and its allies were to learn over the next two decades that in insurgencies, the application of overwhelming military force including air power would not achieve the desired political effect.

Chapter 8
Aerostats to algorithms
2001–2020

Aircraft and air forces have progressively dominated conventional battlefields and oceans in the 20th century and continue to play central roles in these arenas in the early years of the 21st with little sign of immediate change. Military 'interventions' take place regularly and air power is the tool of choice.

It is perhaps something of a paradox that *all* of the aircraft used in the wars of the early 21st century were designed during the Cold War to face similar high-tech opposition. None of them was built to fight insurgents or terrorists in Middle Eastern deserts armed with little more than rifles and home-made roadside bombs.

Recent conflicts have brought us to a place where information is now not only an objective, but a weapon in itself. An entirely new conceptual battle space has been introduced into air warfare—cyber. However, is not cyber simply another way to achieve dominance of the information and intelligence battle space, albeit one with global reach and potentially infinitely faster than any previous form of intelligence or reconnaissance?

9/11, Afghanistan, and Iraq

It might be said that air power has delivered at least four examples of strategically significant air strikes. The first was Pearl Harbor on 7 December 1941 which brought the USA into WW2. The second was the strikes on Hiroshima and Nagasaki which at the very least marked the ending of that war. The third (arguably) was Operation Desert Storm of 1991 in Iraq. The fourth took place on 11 September 2001 in New York and Washington DC when four airliners were hijacked and used as manned missiles.

The immediate response of the USA was to attack Afghanistan where the Taliban government had supported and sustained the 9/11 attackers' terrorist group, al-Qaeda. The situation in Afghanistan, and the Taliban themselves, were the legacy of another failed superpower intervention. In 1979, the Soviet Union had invaded the country, which was in a state of some chaos after a coup against its Soviet-supported government. The Soviets were now to endure their own Vietnam. The original purpose was to stabilize the country and prevent disorder spreading to the Soviet Central Asian states bordering Afghanistan. From 1979 to 1989 air power was used extensively in support of ground forces and independently, often in the deliberate targeting of civilians either as reprisals or warnings. The Soviet Union, itself close to collapse, withdrew in 1989, leaving a puppet Afghan government to stagger on for three years before it fell apart in chaos in 1992. Over one million people had been killed, with many millions more scattered from their homes as refugees. The Taliban, composed largely of former fighters in the anti-Soviet war, had taken power in response to its chaotic aftermath.

Now, in 2001, the USA had intervened. Air power was used extensively to support an insurgent force against the Taliban, the so-called Northern Alliance. US and other NATO special forces were used to call in strikes which devastated ramshackle Taliban formations. A government was installed in Kabul and it seemed that the war was over. At the time, the operation was seen as an exemplary 'low-footprint' ground campaign leveraging overwhelming air power to achieve a satisfactory political result. Unfortunately, there had in fact been no political settlement satisfactory to these conservative Pashtun and other interests in the country which had been represented by the Taliban. A low-level insurgency continued.

Meanwhile, although it had been heavily defeated in the First Gulf War, Iraq maintained a hostile posture towards the USA and its allies, and vice versa. Sanctions hit the country very hard in the 1990s, as did a series of air campaigns (notably Operation Desert Fox in December 1998) designed to contain Iraq's ambitions as a regional power and as a supposed possessor of weapons of mass destruction. In March 2003, US and UK forces, assisted by various coalition partners, attacked Iraq in controversial circumstances, beginning with an air assault on key targets. The term used for this overwhelming display of precision and power was 'shock and awe'. In one sense the shock and awe approach was something of a departure from US bombing rhetoric, being rather more redolent of the kind of policy advocated seventy years previously by Douhet and Trenchard, that of attacking an enemy's *will* to fight rather than his *ability* to do so (see Chapter 3).

On 19 March 2003, the idea that air power could strike directly at an enemy's decision-making heart was taken to its logical conclusion. A series of air strikes by F-117 Stealth aircraft on Dora Farms just outside Baghdad aimed to kill the president of Iraq, Saddam Hussein himself. This was an attempt to use precision and stealth to effect what is called a 'decapitation strike'. Another term might be 'assassination'.

Unfortunately, the attacks succeeded only in killing dozens of civilians, due to an intelligence failure. These strikes demonstrate the problems which will always impact upon even the most precise of air campaigns. The various human and technical means linking the human who selects the target by way of the means of delivery all the way to the target are called the 'kill chain'. This kill chain is subject to two fundamental weaknesses: first, any technical device is subject to failure either of the equipment itself, or of the human operator. Second, the intelligence might simply be wrong. Precision munitions generally hit the target; the question remains, is it the right target?

After a campaign of three weeks the US-led coalition defeated the Iraqi armed forces; it is perhaps enough to state that the USAF alone mounted 41,000 sorties. The Iraqi air force managed not a single mission. However, events were to demonstrate that winning the conventional war was only the first step. By the end of 2004 Iraq was embroiled in a full-scale insurgency. Afghanistan, with a rejuvenated Taliban, followed in 2006.

Contingency operations 2003–2018

In Iraq and Afghanistan, sustained counterinsurgency operations yet again brought the vital importance of CAS to the fore. Yet again, many of these skills had to be relearned. Often, as in previous conflicts, fighter-bombers were called upon. CAS was often delivered by so-called 'organic' air power, which is to say usually attack helicopters, attached to the units being supported. In addition to providing CAS, helicopters were on constant call to provide casualty evacuation, a capability absolutely vital in maintaining the morale of hard-pressed troops. Highly capable transport aircraft maintained an 'air bridge' from the troops' home countries which provided regular opportunities for troops to rotate in and out of the operational theatres. Medical evacuation to hospitals in home countries was also very important, not least for morale. This also allowed for quick reinforcement either of troops or equipment when required, although the bulk of supplies, over 75 per cent, were carried by sea and land.

Needless to say, all of this depended upon having control of the air, although as in southern Vietnam there was the ever-present threat of ground fire usually in the form of guns or anti-tank rockets fired opportunistically against low-flying helicopters. There was a constant intelligence focus on ensuring that man-portable air defence missiles did not fall into the hands of insurgents. In wars with, at best, fragile public support at home, the loss of an air bridge transport aircraft with several hundred soldiers on board to such a missile would have had a profound effect.

In these 'wars amongst the people', intelligence and information were as important as ever. Aircraft were extensively used as intelligence-gathering platforms, from hand-launched drones to helicopters, to satellites and large electronic intelligence-gathering aircraft. These included the RC-135W Rivet Joint aircraft, an adaptation of the Boeing 707 airliner which is commonly used to track and analyse vast quantities of data including mobile-phone traffic. We have seen several times throughout this book that whilst the vocabulary—the equipment—of air power evolves, the basic methods and functions—the grammar—of air power changes little. The function of Rivet Joint and platforms like it is surely nothing more than to 'see the other side of the hill'.

Yet just as in languages old words make unexpected returns, so in air power old ideas come back. The world's first air arm, the French Aerostatic Corps (see Chapter 1), had used tethered balloons as early as 1794 to observe enemy movements during the French Revolutionary Wars. In Afghanistan, tethered aerostats (essentially balloons) were extensively used in a 'force-protection' role, carrying suites of cameras providing imagery to the security teams on the bases they guarded.

The drones come of age

We saw in Chapter 3 that during the 1920s aircraft could be used in places such as Afghanistan, Iraq, or Somalia to replace large numbers of ground troops. This was called 'air policing'. It is remarkable that drones are now being used for the same purposes in the same places. RPAS have several advantages over manned aircraft. They usually have greater range and consequently can loiter over a target for a far longer period than manned aircraft.

Their crews, usually operating in small cabins on air bases often thousands of miles away, can be changed during a mission. There is also no prospect of the aircrew being shot down, unlikely anyway even for manned aircraft where control of the air is unchallenged, but a major advantage when operating over territory without the permission of the country concerned.

As early as 1992 the IDF had deployed RPAS in Lebanon to locate targets and guide weapons (fired from other aircraft) onto them. However Western air forces began to mount highly accurate bombs and rockets on drones very early in the Iraq and Afghan wars. Their ability to loiter undetected for long periods of time on 'overwatch' of a target offered the possibility of conducting precision strikes from RPAS, the first of which took place on 14 November 2001 near Kabul in Afghanistan. Such strikes often take place after crews have observed their targets for days or even weeks, with drones and their operators handing over the targets to replacement aircraft when fuel runs low.

The caveat concerning precision is always present; such weapons may hit the target, but is it the right target? Thousands of such strikes have been carried out, and they have been shown to be accurate insofar as they generally hit the targets that they are aimed at. Of course, as has regularly occurred, the person at whom munitions are directed may not turn out to be the person you want to kill. Targeting is a perennial problem in air warfare and no easier when the target is an individual. Other challenges range from ethics through morality to sovereignty. For example, is there a significant moral difference between a pilot in a manned aircraft being over her target and a pilot sitting in a cabin many thousands of miles away? Is there a moral risk in the ability to kill without the possibility of being killed? Is the violation of sovereignty easier when carried out by what amounts to a radio-controlled aircraft? Is what these aircraft do in fact simply another form of extra-judicial killing? These are issues that are not likely to go away.

It must be remembered that RPAS are indeed controlled. In that respect, they are no different from any other flying weapons system or reconnaissance aircraft. The difference is that the aircrew is not in the aircraft. More serious moral and indeed legal questions will need to be addressed when (and it is 'when') such aircraft are autonomous, in other words when they are capable of utilizing artificial intelligence to make *their own* decisions about strikes. Such aircraft are now in development.

All major air forces now operate significant and growing fleets of RPAS. Huge RPAS such as Global Hawk (with a wing span of 35 metres) conduct missions lasting days, ranging over often hostile territory in much the same way as their Cold War U-2 manned predecessors did. Other designs now in development, such as the BAE Systems Taranis (Figure 13), may well replace the strike aircraft we have today, and be capable of penetrating complex enemy air defence systems. The potential of such capabilities became clearer on 14 September 2019, when about a dozen drones (and some cruise missiles) breached the

13. A Royal Air Force Typhoon fighter next to a BAE Systems Taranis drone.

sophisticated US-supplied Saudi-Arabian air defence system and struck oil refineries at Abqaiq with a significant effect on Saudi oil production.

Over the last half-decade small units of soldiers have been issued with battlefield drones to be used at the lowest tactical level. Some of these are smaller than a person's hand. One example is the Black Hornet nano-UAV, used by individual soldiers literally to see what is around a corner or on the other side of a building. Insurgents and non-state actors also use relatively low-cost but sophisticated systems in both reconnaissance and attack roles. During the battle to retake the Iraqi city of Mosul from the so-called 'Islamic State' (IS) in 2017–18, IS fighters used small quadcopter drones, available commercially for about $650, to spot Iraqi, US, and other anti-IS coalition soldiers and drop grenades on them. Interestingly this was the first time since the Korean War that US troops had come under attack from the air.

A return to high-end conflict?

In their early stages, the wars in Afghanistan and Iraq seemed straightforward military successes. Indeed they were; at least until political realities on the ground intervened. Unfortunately, Western strategists ignored the dictum of their guru Carl von Clausewitz concerning war being a political act. There had been tactical successes, but there had not been a policy to drive the necessary combination of ends, ways, and means to produce success. There was, in other words, no effective strategy.

As in Vietnam, so in Iraq and Afghanistan. Israel found in 2006 that air power might well cause extensive destruction of its enemy (on this occasion Lebanese Hezbollah) as well as its heartland and infrastructure, but this did not stop Hezbollah, still a viable force, from plausibly claiming victory. Despite the onslaught, Hezbollah retained considerable military capability and remained an effective political actor. The promise of air power to deliver an easy victory was also broken over Libya in 2011, where NATO air power easily defeated Muammar Gaddafi's forces only for the country to descend into a long night of chaos. Western military force, specifically air power, would certainly ensure the defeat of the poorly equipped and led Libyan armed forces. What it could not do, however, was ensure a satisfactory political result. Further, the Libyan campaign served to illustrate the limitations of non-US NATO air forces. More than half of the air strikes and well over half of the enabling activity, such as reconnaissance and air-to-air refuelling, were carried out by US aircraft.

Nonetheless, one message delivered firmly to the adversaries, if not yet enemies, of the West, China and Russia, was that they were not likely to defeat Western, or particularly US, air forces *in the air*. Consequently they have adopted the approach taken by Egypt after the 1967 debacle, focusing on anti-aircraft capabilities which, at the time of writing, seriously threaten US dominance in an air campaign. China has implemented an air–sea strategy built around hypersonic anti-ship missiles. It is called 'anti-access, area denial' (A2AD) and is intended to counter aircraft carrier groups. One difficulty for Western air arms is that since the early 1990s, the continuing series of contingency, peacekeeping, and counterinsurgency operations has meant that training and preparation for high-end air combat has often suffered.

The vast resources of states are now, as ever, applied to new technology at the 'high end' of warfare in a constant cycle of one-upmanship. At the time of writing in 2020, 'information dominance' and 'network-centric warfare' are current buzzwords. They are not in fact new concepts or terms—they have been around for decades. What is new is the ability to make them happen. In due course it may well be that these capabilities will require a new set of theories and doctrines; indeed, in the cyber domain, new thinking and doctrine is already being applied.

Cyber and the information domain

In early 2017, Lieutenant-General William Bender, Chief Information Officer of the USAF, said: 'Not a thing that we do, not a mission that we have is not dependent on the ones and the zeros, the connectedness required to be effective. The enemy knows that and the enemy gets a vote.' Clearly, Syria's air defenders during Operation Orchard (Box 5) discovered this the hard way.

This is not a treatise on cyber-warfare (although some air forces see cyber as a suitable role for them). The USAF alone in the form of its Twenty-Fourth Air Force—its dedicated cyber unit—has no fewer than 14,000 airmen and airwomen dedicated to this form of conflict. The cyber domain is becoming central to the way that air power is being viewed now and into the future.

New generations of aircraft are being seen as information systems that are designed to be completely integrated with each other. It is difficult to understate the importance of maintaining secure data links between different aircraft (now often called 'aerial platforms'), the satellite systems they depend upon for navigation and targeting, and ground support or control.

If those links are broken or compromised, the aircraft—whether manned or unmanned—become far less capable or indeed entirely incapable. In December 2011, a highly secret US RQ-170 drone appeared to have had its controlling data link severed by Iranian hackers, who then took control of the craft and landed it at an Iranian airfield. It is for that reason that cyber capabilities are so potentially dangerous. Hacking of aircraft and computer systems to break or disrupt data links is one matter, the deliberate introduction of carefully designed computer viruses is another.

Information dominance is now considered to be a key element in contemporary conflict. The most expensive weapons system in

Box 5 The invisible raid: Operation Orchard 2007

For decades Israel has acted to prevent hostile states from developing a nuclear capability. On 7 June 1981, Israeli bombers breached Iraqi air defences and destroyed the Osirak nuclear reactor under construction a few miles south-east of Baghdad.

Syrian air defences are now rather more formidable than those deployed by Iraq in 1981. In the early morning of 7 September 2007, two squadrons of the IAF's elite 'Hammer' Wing bombed Syria's only—and highly secret—nuclear reactor at Al Kibar, near the town of Deir ez-Zor in the deserts of eastern Syria. Two hours later, the thirty or so Israeli F-15s and F-16s returned to base. The first the Syrians knew of an air raid was when the morning shift arrived at the wrecked reactor.

The raiders were not stealth aircraft, yet the IAF had still managed to defeat the sophisticated Syrian IADS. The only unusual feature of the evening for the Syrians was that at one moment their radar screens seemed to be swamped with unidentified contacts. This appeared simply to be a glitch, as the screens quickly returned to normal.

The weapon the Israelis used to neutralize their opponents' early warning system was a computer virus. This was introduced to the Syrian IADS through an, as yet unknown, vulnerability, perhaps a human agent handled by Mossad, perhaps a technical mechanism or simple hack. It ensured that the Syrian controllers saw only what their Israeli adversaries wanted them to see. The Israelis had hijacked the Syrian IADS for the duration of the raid, codenamed Operation Orchard. It eliminated the Syrian nuclear programme and removed any ambition for nuclear weaponry. This was the use of aircraft in its strategic strike role at its most efficient and effective. Orchard is an indicator of how high-end air warfare is being thought about and indeed conducted as you read this book.

history, the Lockheed Martin F-35 Lightning II, is often described as a fifth-generation fighter (the first four generations were progressively faster and more capable). Its advocates claim it to be more than a mere fighter. Hugely powerful computers and sensors integrate information from a number of internal and external sources. If all these systems can be made to work together, for the first time a pilot will have a complete picture of both the air and ground battle space projected onto a virtual reality visor in his or her helmet. Data links are designed to enable the pilot's situational awareness to be communicated widely to other aircraft and indeed land and maritime platforms.

One view is that this combination of situational awareness, stealth, and other capabilities has produced a 'first-generation information and decision-making superiority flying combat system'. One commentator has rightly quipped that 'this is a claim somewhat redolent of Douhet's Battleplane', a multi-role air dominance machine described in the 1927 edition of *Command of the Air*. When the French air force attempted that concept in the 1930s, it was a total failure. The history of air power is full of claims of step changes which are rarely justified. Certainly, these new capabilities also represent new vulnerabilities; technologically adroit enemies will be making huge efforts to intercept, disrupt, or block those ones and zeros which carry that crucial data.

Chapter 9
Per ardua ad astra?

We are only at the beginning of the age of the drone and many, many possibilities are mooted for their future. The idea of unmanned fighters making air combat and manoeuvring decisions in microseconds is now thought to be a matter of, at most, two decades away. Will fighter pilots exist then? Will aircrew in combat aircraft become a thing of the past? Some airmen of today argue that a machine is unlikely to reproduce the 'airmindedness' of a human pilot in the aircraft. Others point out that most aircraft can be flown from the ground even as matters stand, including the F-35. Indeed, they argue that without the constraints of what they call 'wetware' (the human pilot), the performance of aircraft will improve; computers do not require oxygen, heat, or parachutes.

New types of roles are being considered for old types of aircraft; for example, redesigning large transport aircraft such as the C-17 Globemasters as 'motherships' deploying drones, rather like airborne aircraft carriers. Other air power visionaries foresee swarms of nano-drones under the control of individual operators conducting attack, reconnaissance, or even fighter missions. Hypersonic long-range anti-aircraft weapons have already been deployed, and directed energy weapons, such as lethal lasers, have been tested. These will surely change air combat. For a start they may render pointless the manoeuvrability of aircraft. There is no evasion of a weapon which travels at the speed of light. When I asked a pilot with extensive experience on the F-22 (a fifth-generation fighter) what he thought a sixth-generation fighter would look like, he replied: 'it could be manned, unmanned; it could be a swarm of nano-bots; on reflection you know, it could be an algorithm.' Whatever it is, the function it will fulfil is the same as ever—to ensure control of the air to enable reconnaissance, attack, and mobility.

So *plus ça change, plus c'est la même chose* for much in air warfare? There has been at least one major change over the decades since the end of the Cold War—the political effects caused by collateral damage. This, coupled with vastly increased public awareness as the result of an ever-more pervasive media, has given far greater prominence to the law of armed conflict. Events in the Syrian Civil War, where air power has played a considerable if not decisive role, have demonstrated that some countries take their obligations in the international law of armed conflict rather more seriously than others.

Air power and air forces are not the same. Air forces do not and never have, despite their claims, owned air power. Navies and army air elements are no longer, as Douhet called them, mere 'auxiliaries'. Some highly effective defence forces, such as that of Israel, do not have truly independent air forces at all. Armies, navies, and marine corps (the US Marine Corps operates an air arm far bigger and better armed than the RAF), as well as coastguards and other civilian agencies such as the US Central Intelligence Agency, all deploy aircraft for military or defensive ends. They always have and they always will. However, it is certain that there is still a strong institutional drive towards independence on the part of existing air forces. So in the 1920s (or indeed before), so today, there is often considerable rivalry and squabbling between all branches of armed forces for limited resources.

In 2018, the Royal Air Force, the world's oldest air force, marked its one hundredth anniversary. Today, major air forces such as the RAF (whose motto is *per ardua ad astra*, through adversity to the stars) and its much larger cousin the US Air Force consider themselves *aerospace* forces. To a great degree they see their future operating in space, cyberspace as we have seen, and airspace. 'The air ocean and its endless outer space extension are one and indivisible and should be controlled by a single homogenous force'; so said Alexander de Seversky. The men and women of today's air forces agree. Nonetheless, questions are still regularly raised about the continuing viability of air forces as separate military institutions.

Two factors might militate against the de facto (as opposed to formal) independence of air forces. First, there is the ever-more integrated nature of modern military forces. Second, there is the money. With the burgeoning costs of such platforms as the F-35 (well over $120 million each), or the P-8 maritime patrol aircraft (more than $250 million each), a phenomenon known as 'structural disarmament' takes effect—the reduction of a force's size due to cost. Air forces can afford ever fewer numbers of aircraft. However, a reduction in the number of airframes does not necessarily equate to a reduction in capability. Contemporary aircraft have capabilities that far exceed their immediate predecessors.

Leading military historian Martin van Creveld points out that the US Air Force shot down its last enemy aircraft in 1999 (over Kosovo), although a US Navy fighter shot down a Syrian aircraft in 2017. The USAF might, however, reply that the last time US ground forces came under lethal enemy air attack was in April 1953 (during the Korean War); this fact alone is surely a testament to its success in maintaining control of the air against enemy air forces.

The RAF has not destroyed an enemy plane in air-to-air combat since 1948 when a Spitfire downed two Egyptian aircraft attacking its base in Palestine. It is worth noting that British Harriers—a few of them piloted by RAF officers—did shoot down twenty-three Argentine aircraft during the Falklands War of 1982, but they were owned and operated by the Royal Navy. Van Creveld argues that 'assuming that 21st century [wars] will be mainly of the low intensity kind…there probably is no compelling case for independent air power at all'. It may well not at all be a safe assumption that future conflict will be 'low intensity'. Another air power scholar, Robert Farley, has argued that the formation of separate air forces such as the USAF was a mistake and that now they are simply obsolete and air power roles should be devolved to the other military services.

Whether the structures of air forces remain similar, or change radically, one thing is certain—aircraft of one kind or another will continue to be vital components of any military operation. The words of Douhet still resound: 'To conquer[,] Command of the Air means victory. To be beaten in the air means defeat, and acceptance of whatever terms the enemy may be pleased to impose.' Whatever the limitations of air forces, air power is critical to most if not all military operations today. In 2014, USAF General Frank Gorenc said that 'Airpower is like oxygen. When you have enough, you don't have to think about it, when you don't have enough it's the only thing you think about.'

On the other hand, having command of the air carries with it temptations to rely upon air power in trying to solve complex problems. In the absence of a workable overall strategy this will fail; this is a matter which was not lost upon the earliest visionaries. H. G. Wells published his *War in the Air* in 1909, six years after the Wright brothers had first flown in a powered aircraft. He describes a London thirty years after its devastation from the air. Through the silent ruins walk a boy and an older man:

'But why did they start the War?' asks the boy.

'They couldn't help themselves', his uncle replies. "'Avin' them airships made them'.

References

Chapter 1: Foundations

Carl Barrow, 'Annual Address to the Marine Corps Association', Proceedings, 1980.

Giulio Douhet, *The Command of the Air*, ed. Joseph Harahan and Richard Kohn (University of Alabama Press, 2009), p. 9.

Giulio Douhet, 'Probable Aspects of Future War', in Joseph Harahan and Richard Kohn (eds), *The Command of the Air* (University of Alabama Press, 2009), p. 119.

David Edgerton, *England and the Aeroplane* (Penguin, 2013), p. 148.

Robin Higham, 'The Arab Air Forces', in Robin Higham and Stephen Harris (eds), *Why Air Forces Fail: The Anatomy of Defeat* (University Press of Kentucky, 2006), pp. 71–98.

Reginald Pound and Geoffrey Harmsworth, *Northcliffe* (Cassell, 1959), p. 325.

Chapter 2: Beginnings: the First World War 1914–1918

Sebastian Cox and Peter Gray, *Air Power History: Turning Points from Kitty Hawk to Kosovo* (Frank Cass, 2002), p. 94.

Arthur Gould Lee, *No Parachute: A Fighter Pilot in World War I* (Grub Street, 2013), pp. 293–4.

Nick Lloyd, *Passchendaele* (Penguin, 2017), p. 116.

Chapter 3: Theory and practice: the interwar years 1919–1939

Giulio Douhet, *The Command of the Air*, ed. Joseph Harahan and Richard Kohn (University of Alabama Press, 2009), pp. 57 and 61.

National Archives, AIR 10/1214 (1920), 'Results of Air Raids on Germany 1 Jan.–11 Nov. 1918'.

Alan Stephens (ed.), *The War in the Air, 1914–1994* (Air University Press, 2001), p. 61.

Chapter 4: The Second World War: air operations in the West

Stephen Bungay, *The Most Dangerous Enemy* (Aurum Press, 2000), pp. 64, 69.

Winston Churchill, *The Second World War*, Vol. 4: *The Hinge of Fate* (Houghton Mifflin, 1950).

Colin D. Heaton and Anne-Marie Lewis, *The German Aces Speak: World War II though the Eyes of the Luftwaffe's Most Important Commanders* (Zenith, 2011), p. 91.

Life Magazine, 28 February 1949, p. 47.

Richard Overy, *The Bombing War* (Penguin, 2014), p. 59ff.

US War Department Field Manual 100-20; *Command and Employment of Air Power (1943)* chapter 1, section 1, paragraph 1.

Chapter 5: The Second World War: the air war in the Pacific

Conrad Crane, *Bombs, Cities and Civilians: American Air Power Strategy in WW2* (University Press of Kansas, 1993), p. 133.

Colonel (Ret'd) Joseph Sweeney, US Air Force Museum Podcast Series, 'B29 Bocksar', August 2015, available at <http://www.nationalmuseum.af.mil/Portals/7/av/B-29_bockscar_70th_anniversary.mp3?ver=2015-08-28-131128-853>.

Chapter 6: Cold War 1945–1982

Mark Clodfelter, *The Limits of Air Power* (Free Press, 1989), p. 11.

Eliezar Cohen, *Israel's Best Defense* (Airlife, 1994), p. 193.

Arthur Miller, *Einstein, Picasso: Space, Time and the Beauty that Causes Havoc* (Basic Books, 2001) p. 172.

Colonel John Warden, *The Air Campaign: Planning for Combat* (Brassey's, 1989), p. 119.

Chapter 7: The apotheosis of air power 1983–2001

Mark Clodfelter, *The Limits of Air Power* (Free Press, 1989), p. 203.

Tony Mason, *Air Power: A Centennial Appraisal* (Brassey's, 2003), pp. 152–66.

Thomas C. Schelling, *Arms and Influence* (Yale University Press, 2008), p. 146.

Chapter 8: Aerostats to algorithms 2001–2020

General William Bender, 'Address to Carnegie Council', Washington DC, 8 March 2017, available at <https://www.carnegiecouncil.org/studio/multimedia/20170308-breaking-barriers-the-united-states-air-force-and-the-future-of-cyberpower>.

Ross Mahoney, 'Commentary—A Rose by Any Other Name', 9 October 2016, available at <https://balloonstodrones.com/2016/10/09/commentary-a-rose-by-any-other-name/>. Robin Laird came up with the optimistic description of the F-35 as a 'first-generation information dominance' machine.

Chapter 9: *Per ardua ad astra?*

Alexander De Seversky, 'On Strategic Organisation', *Air Force*, June 1958, vol. 41, no. 6, pp. 83–8.

Giulio Douhet, *The Command of the Air*, ed. Joseph Harahan and Richard Kohn (University of Alabama Press, 2009), p. 28.

General Frank Gorenc, farewell address as Commander Allied Air Command, and Director Joint Air Power Competence Centre, August 2016, available at <https://www.japcc.org/nato-air-power-last-word/>.

Martin van Creveld, 'The Rise and Fall of Air Power', in John Andreas Olsen (ed.), *A History of Air Warfare* (Potomac Books, 2010), pp. 369–70.

Further reading

Bergman, Ronen, *Rise and Kill First: The Secret History of Israel's Targeted Assassinations* (Random House, 2018).

Bergstrom, Christer, *The Battle of Britain: An Epic Conflict Revisited* (Casemate, 2015).

Biddle, Tami Davis, *Rhetoric and Reality in Air Warfare: The Evolution of American and British Ideas about Strategic Bombing 1914-1945* (Princeton University Press, 2009).

Bishop, Patrick, *Bomber Boys: Fighting Back 1940-1945* (Harper, 2011).

Bishop, Patrick, *Wings: The RAF at War 1912-2012* (Atlantic Books, 2012).

British Bombing Survey Unit (with forewords by Michael Beecham and John Huston, and additional material by Sebastian Cox), *The Strategic Air War against Germany 1939-45* (Frank Cass, 1998).

Bronk, Justin, *Maximum Value from the F35: Harnessing Transformational Fifth-Generation Capabilities for the UK Military* (RUSI, 2016).

Budiansky, Stephen, *Air Power from Kitty Hawk to Gulf War II: A History of the People, Ideas and Machinery that Transformed War in the Century of Flight* (Viking, 2003).

Bungay, Stephen, *Most Dangerous Enemy: A History of the Battle of Britain* (Aurum Press, 2000).

Clodfelter, Mark, *The Limits of Air Power: The American Bombing of North Vietnam* (Free Press, 1989).

Coates, Kenneth A. and Redfern, Jerry, *Eternal Harvest: The Legacy of American Bombs in Laos* (ThingsAsian Press, 2013).

Cohen, Eliezar, *Israel's Best Defense* (Airlife, 1994).

Coram, Robert, *Boyd: The Fighter Pilot who Changed the Art of War* (Little, Brown and Company, 2003).

Corum, James S., *The Luftwaffe: Creating the Operational Air War* (University Press of Kansas, 1997).

Coutelle, Jean-Marie Joseph, *Sur l'aérostat employé aux armées de Sambre-et-Meuse et du Rhin* (Chapelet, 1829).

Cox, Sebastian and Gray, Peter, *Air Power History: Turning Points from Kitty Hawk to Kosovo* (Frank Cass, 2002).

De Villiers, Marc, *Les Aérostiers militaires en Egypte* (Camproger, 1901).

Douhet, Giulio, *The Command of the Air*, ed. Joseph Harahan and Richard Kohn (University of Alabama Press, 2009).

Edgerton, David, *England and the Aeroplane* (Penguin, 2013).

Ehlers, Robert S., *The Mediterranean Air War: Airpower and Allied Victory in World War II* (University Press of Kansas, 2015).

Farley, Robert J., *Grounded: The Case for Abolishing the United States Air Force* (University Press of Kentucky, 2015).

Frankland, Noble, *Bomber Offensive: The Devastation of Europe* (Macdonald, 1970).

Gates, David, *Sky Wars: A History of Military Aerospace Power* (Reaktion Books, 2003).

Gates, David and Jones, Ben, *Air Power in the Maritime Environment: The World Wars* (Routledge, 2016).

Gray, Peter, *The Leadership, Direction and Legitimacy of the RAF Bomber Offensive from Inception to 1945* (Birmingham War Studies, 2012).

Gray, Peter, *Air Warfare: History, Theory and Practice* (Bloomsbury, 2016).

Hallion, Richard P., *Taking Flight: Inventing the Aerial Age from Antiquity through the First World War* (Oxford University Press, 2003).

Hamilton-Paterson, James, *Marked for Death* (Head of Zeus, 2015).

Hastings, Max, *Bomber Command* (Pan reprints, 2010).

Heaton, Colin D. and Lewis, Anne-Marie, *The German Aces Speak: World War II through the Eyes of the Luftwaffe's Most Important Commanders* (Zenith, 2011).

Heuser, Beatrice, *The Evolution of Strategy* (Cambridge University Press, 2011).

Higham, Robin, Greenwood, John T., and Hardesty, Von (eds), *Russian Aviation and Air Power in the Twentieth Century* (Frank Cass, 1998).

Higham, Robin and Harris, Stephen J. (eds), *Why Air Forces Fail* (University Press of Kentucky, 2002).

Kennedy, Paul, *Engineers of Victory* (Penguin, 2014).

Lacroix, Desire, *Les Aérostiers militaires du Château de Meudon* (Auguste Ghio, 1885).

Lardas, Mark, *World War I Seaplane and Aircraft Carriers* (Osprey, 2016).

Lee, Arthur Gould, *No Parachute: A Classic Account of War in the Air* (Grub Street, 2013).

Lloyd, Nick, *Passchendaele* (Penguin, 2017).

Mason, Herbert Molloy, *The Rise of the Luftwaffe 1918–1940* (Endeavour Press, 2016).

Mason, Tony, *Air Power: A Centennial Appraisal* (Brassey's, 2nd edn, 2002).

Miller, Arthur, *Einstein, Picasso: Space, Time and the Beauty that Causes Havoc* (Basic Books, 2001).

Miller, Russell, *Boom: The Life of Viscount Trenchard, Father of the Royal Air Force* (Weidenfeld and Nicolson, 2016).

Mitter, Rann, *China's War with Japan 1937–1945: The Struggle for Survival* (Allen Lane, 2013).

O'Brien, Phillips Payson, *How the War was Won* (Cambridge University Press, 2015).

Olsen, John Andreas (ed.), *A History of Air Power* (Potomac Books, 2007).

Olsen, John Andreas (ed.), *Global Air Power* (Potomac Books, 2011).

Olsen, John Andreas (ed.), *Air Power Reborn* (Naval Institute Press, 2015).

Olsen, John Andreas (ed.), *Air Power Applied* (Naval Institute Press, 2017).

Orange, Vincent, *Tedder: Quietly in Command* (Routledge, 2004).

Orange, Vincent, *Dowding of Fighter Command* (Grub Street, 2008).

Overy, Richard, *The Air War 1939–1945* (Papermac, 1987).

Overy, Richard, *The Battle of Britain: Myths and Reality* (Penguin, 2010).

Overy, Richard, *The Bombing War* (Penguin, 2013).

Owen, Robert C., *Air Mobility* (University of Nebraska Press, 2013).

Preston, Paul, *The Destruction of Guernica* (Harper Press, 2013).

Ray, John, *The Battle of Britain: Dowding and the First Victory* (Cassell, 2000).

Renfrew, Barry, *Wings of Empire* (History Press, 2015).

Ritchie, Sebastian, *The RAF: Small Wars and Insurgencies in the Middle East, 1919-1939* (Centre for Air Power Studies, 2011).

Rubin, Uzi, *Israel's Air and Missile Defence During the 2014 Gaza War* (Begin-Sadat Center for Strategic Studies, Mideast Security and Policy Study No. 111, 2015).

Schelling, Thomas C., *Arms and Influence* (Yale University Press, 2008).

Seversky, Alexander de, *Victory through Air Power* (Simon and Schuster, 1942).

Stephens, Alan, *The War in the Air 1914-1994* (Air University Press, 2002).

Subramanian, Arjan, *India's Wars* (HarperCollins India, 2016).

Tillman, Barrett, *Whirlwind: The Air War against Japan 1942-45* (Simon and Schuster, 2010).

United States Department of Defense, *The United States Strategic Bombing Surveys: European War and Pacific War in WW2, Conventional Bombing and the Atomic Bombings of Hiroshima and Nagasaki* (Department of Defense, original report, 1945).

United States War Department Field Manual 100-20; *Command and Employment of Air Power (1943).*

Van Creveld, Martin, *The Age of Air Power* (Public Affairs, 2011).

Van Creveld, Martin, Canby, Steven L., and Brower, Kenneth, S., *Air Power and Maneuver Warfare* (University Press of the Pacific, 2002).

Warden, Colonel John, *The Air Campaign: Planning for Combat* (Brassey's, 1989).

Wells, H. G., *The War of the Worlds & The War in the Air* (Wordsworth, 2017).

Wills, Colin, *Unmanned Combat Air Systems in Future Warfare* (Palgrave Macmillan, 2015).

Wilson, Kevin, *Blood and Fears* (Weidenfeld and Nicolson, 2016).

Zaloga, Steven J., *Operation Pointblank 1944: Defeating the Luftwaffe* (Osprey, 2011).

Index